The Gift of Betrayal

Also by Eve A. Wood, M.D.

The Stop Anxiety Now Kit:
A Powerful Program of Easy-to-Implement Tools
to Stop Anxiety and Transform Your Life

10 Steps to Take Charge of Your Emotional Life:
Overcoming Anxiety, Distress, and Depression
Through Whole-Person Healing

There's Always Help; There's Always Hope:
An Award-Winning Psychiatrist Shows You
How to Heal Your Body, Mind, and Spirit

What Am I Feeling, and What Does It Mean?:
A Kit for Self-Growth and Healthy Relationships

All of the above are available at your
local bookstore, or may be ordered by visiting:

Hay House USA: **www.hayhouse.com®**
Hay House Australia: **www.hayhouse.com.au**
Hay House UK: **www.hayhouse.co.uk**
Hay House South Africa: **www.hayhouse.co.za**
Hay House India: **www.hayhouse.co.in**

The Gift of Betrayal

How to Heal Your Life When Your World Explodes

Eve A. Wood, M.D.

An *In One*® Series Book

HAY HOUSE, INC.
Carlsbad, California • New York City
London • Sydney • Johannesburg
Vancouver • Hong Kong • New Delhi

Published and distributed in the United States by: Hay House, Inc.: www.hayhouse.com • *Published and distributed in Australia by:* Hay House Australia Pty. Ltd.: www.hayhouse.com.au • *Published and distributed in the United Kingdom by:* Hay House UK, Ltd.: www.hayhouse.co.uk • *Published and distributed in the Republic of South Africa by:* Hay House SA (Pty), Ltd.: www.hayhouse.co.za • *Distributed in Canada by:* Raincoast: www.raincoast.com • *Published in India by:* Hay House Publishers India: www.hayhouse.co.in

Editorial supervision: Jill Kramer • *Design:* Nick C. Welch

Library of Congress Cataloging-in-Publication Data

Wood, Eve A.
   The gift of betrayal : how to heal your life when your world explodes / Eve A. Wood.
     p. cm.
   ISBN 978-1-4019-1849-1 (tradepaper : alk. paper) 1. Women--Psychology. 2. Betrayal. 3. Man-woman relationships. 4. Adjustment (Psychology) I. Title.
   HQ1206.W8928 2009
   155.6'33--dc22   2008051462

ISBN: 978-1-4019-1849-1

12 11 10 09   4 3 2 1
1st edition, May 2009

Printed in the United States of America

*To my awesome sisters of choice without whom
I would never have gotten to this place:*

*Ann-Marie Chiasson
Amy Lederman
Victoria Maizes
Debbie Schraeger
Patty Vallance*

In reverence, gratitude, and love.

Author's Note

Many of the stories in this book are true accounts in which the names and identifying details have been changed to protect confidentiality. Others are composites drawn from years of clinical work. The latter are true to the spirit of teaching, although not to the experience of any particular person.

Contents

Introduction

GRASPING THE GIFT OF BETRAYAL

We have all heard the expressions *Every cloud has a silver lining, There's light at the end of the tunnel,* and *God doesn't give you anything more than you can handle.* But when your world explodes—when your lover, life partner, or spouse betrays you . . . when your picture-perfect life turns to ashes—those truisms become platitudes. They sound hollow. They just don't ring true.

I've worked with many women who have lived through horrendous, gut-wrenching, life-altering betrayals. I've helped them climb out of the pits of despair, hopelessness, self-loathing, grief, powerlessness, and pain. We've raged, joked, laughed, and cried together as we've explored questions such as:

- *Why me?*
- *How could he have done this?*
- *Who is he anyway?*
- *How could I have missed it?*
- *What is wrong with me?*
- *How did I get here?*
- *Why do I keep choosing people like this?*
- *Is anyone really trustworthy?*
- *Will I ever be able to trust again?*

Together, we have journeyed through the pain, the history, the lessons, the acceptance, and the transformation. And everyone I've had the opportunity to work with has proved the truisms . . . to be *true!* And when *my* life exploded in betrayal . . . I did the same thing.

There's hope, healing, and great joy available to—and waiting for—each and every one of us who has been betrayed. But we need to grasp the *gift* in betrayal in order to experience it. We must grasp it intellectually—understand it, make sense of it, and learn from it. And we must do so physically—seize it, step into it, and make it our story. If my patients and I can do that, so can *you!*

I'll start by telling you my story and share some of my patients' experiences later on as you and I step into healing work together. Although I wrote this book for women in heterosexual relationships, many of its teachings will help you if you're a gay man or woman, or a heterosexual man who has been betrayed. You will obviously need to change the "he" to "she" and the "she" to "he" as you read the examples (and you'll notice that some of the chapters do apply exclusively to women and male-female relationships).

My Story

Once upon a time, long, long ago—when I believed in "happily ever after"—I got married. I was 23 years old, a second-year medical student, and in love for the first time. Peter (not his real name), the object of my affection, was a man four months older than I and a year ahead of me in medical school. Not only were we both students, but we'd both been perpetual students since preschool. After spending a mere 16 months with the man whom I thought was the answer to my prayers, I stood before my family, friends, and rabbi, in the synagogue of my childhood. I pledged to take Peter to be my husband. I vowed to love, honor, and cherish him in sickness and in health as long as we both would live. But I had no idea what I was doing!

I thought I knew myself. And I thought I knew *him*. My mother encouraged me to marry Peter after seven months of courtship. He'd just moved into my apartment, and she was worried. "He'll live with you out of wedlock forever if you don't get married right away," she said. And I thought *that* would be a problem. I was a naïve, starry-eyed good girl. So I got engaged . . . and I really thought I was doing the right thing. . . .

Soon after my engagement, I became really depressed— not clinically depressed, but I couldn't stop crying for days. I didn't know what was wrong with me. *I should be happier than I've ever been in my entire life,* I thought. *What could possibly be wrong?* I talked to my friends and sought counseling. My tearfulness was chalked up to hormones and to other (what I now realize were) ridiculous, nondescript causes. No one said to me, "Maybe your body is trying to tell you something about this marriage plan. Maybe you ought to get out." And, not realizing what I now know about mind-body interactions, I plowed ahead with the wedding plans my mother was making. I was being compliant and doing what I'd always done. I didn't know any better. *None of us can act beyond our wisdom.*

Throughout my engagement, I was episodically unsettled. My fiancé and I had some fabulous times together, but we also fought with each other. This was a brand-new experience for me. I hate conflict and had always avoided it whenever possible. I was often hurt by Peter's words and actions. Yet we seemed to be working things out. But I didn't really know what working it out involved. My parents *never* disagreed about anything in front of their children. They believed they were setting a good example for us.

As a child and young adult, I always needed to have goals—to know where I was going and what I was meant to do to get there. Perhaps, my illusion of control was one of the things that kept me sane in my dysfunctional household. Anyway, knowing that I was marrying the man I was sup-posed to marry kept me going; the good times I had with him reinforced my conscious belief that he and I would live happily ever after. And my conscious belief probably kept making me try to make the impossible occur.

My marriage plan didn't unfold like I thought it would. By the time I finished my psychiatry residency training, I was the proud parent of a colicky baby boy. And within less than three years, my husband and I were coparenting two sons. While I desperately wanted children, the roller-coaster experience of my courtship didn't settle down. The stress and upheaval continued, and I kept trying to "work it out" no matter what came my way.

I must admit that I was deeply joyful at times. I had fun with my spouse and had a rewarding practice and wonder-ful kids. But I couldn't count on or trust my husband to be supportive in a consistent way. I often felt undermined by him and disappointed, unhappy, overwhelmed, confused, and deeply dissatisfied. I pursued therapy and counsel-ing over the years . . . as did he. But the problems seemed to escalate.

Miserable things would happen. He would apologize and commit to changing, but he continued violating my trust. I kept fixing problems and putting out fires. I was hoping he would change, but I lived in dread and fear. I felt like I was living with a Dr. Jekyll–and–Mr. Hyde character. His support would turn to attack without warning.

On the occasion of my 24th wedding anniversary, my husband and I had four children, ages 9 to 19 . . . and we slept in separate rooms. I felt ill in his company. I was in a lot of pain . . . and then my world exploded.

I was confronted with irrefutable evidence that Peter was living a double life. He was involved in activities that rock the foundation of what it means to honor, cherish, and support a wife (for legal reasons, I'm unable to go into the specific details of what he did, but the magnitude of the betrayal was truly shocking). My illusion of being able to make my marriage work was shattered. I was devastated. I told my husband to move out. And . . . after 27 years of trying to make the unworkable work, I filed for divorce.

I was facing a bombshell, a fractured plane in the earth of my life wider than the Grand Canyon. My whole adult life had been spent trying to build a family and a future with the man who had betrayed me. We had four children together. Over the years, my parents, friends, colleagues, and other relatives had stepped in to help my husband deal with one challenge after another. We'd all trusted, sacrificed, and invested our resources and ourselves in helping him. But we'd hoped for more. And I'd just come to discover that much of my life was a lie. My husband had been putting me in danger. It began to sink in. I could have *died!* My children could have been left without a mother. And all the while my husband had been engaging in this behavior, he'd been telling me that I wasn't supportive enough of *him!*

If you're reading this book, you've probably been there, too. You know what it feels like to be betrayed, to have your life shattered, to see your dreams go up in smoke. What would, or did, you do? How do you heal your life when your world explodes?

You have a choice. You can see this betrayal as a curse or a blessing. You can make it about him, or you can make it about you. You can be the victim, or you can take charge. You can blame him, or you can learn about yourself and move on. You can grow or shrink. You can heal your life or shrivel up and die. You can choose joy, light, and love . . . or remain bitter and alone.

I chose to see the gift in my betrayal experience. I opted to learn from it and used it as an opportunity to create the life I've always wanted to have. And I'm here to tell you that I've never been happier. I thank God for putting that final nail in the coffin of my prior marriage. I'm creating my heart's desire. I'm currently involved with a man who lights up my life. I'm laughing and singing more than I have for years. There's a lightness in my step, a giggle in my voice, and a whole lot more lovin' going on than I ever dreamed I'd experience. Passion and pleasure have replaced my pain and perseverance. And I'm thrilled to be free! I've grasped the gift of betrayal, and *you* can, too. Your betrayal can become your liberation. In these pages, I intend to show you how to make that happen.

Most books about betrayal focus on forgiveness, on forgiving the offender and yourself. But I think the attention on forgiving is misguided. When you've been burned, you need to treat your wound. You must figure out how you got scorched in the first place and learn how to heal. Then you may begin forgiving yourself, and *only* yourself. As you move forward, you'll determine how to deal with the aggressor who put your hand in the fire in the first place. Only as you begin to recover and transcend your pain will you be able to start to forgive the perpetrator. You can't do so sooner. That would be like looking over your shoulder while you're trying to walk forward: you'd likely trip, fall, and maybe even break your neck. It's not about *him;* your healing is about—and for—*you.*

To heal your life, you need to step fully into it. You deserve a glorious future, and I intend to show you how to get there. The first step in achieving that future is allowing yourself to believe it's possible for you. So start telling yourself it is . . . and begin the process. You'll be amazed by the places you'll go!

How to Use This Book

I've organized this book around 14 key questions or lessons involved in grasping the gift of betrayal. My patients, and my own life journey, have taught me that these teachings are among the most crucial ones in healing your life when your world explodes. Each key lesson is a separate chapter, and you'll find a series of important concepts that interrelate. With *The Gift of Betrayal,* I've written the book that I wish *I* had been able to read many years ago. Perhaps it would have helped me make sense of my experience and would have saved me a lot of heartache and pain. I hope and pray that it serves that purpose in your life. You can find your unique path to wholeness. You needn't suffer so much!

Here are the 14 key questions or lessons. I urge you to grasp them, learn them, and make them your own:

1. What is betrayal, how does it feel, and where can it take you?

2. You have a choice: do you seize your power or become the victim?

3. Could you have been married to (or involved with) a sociopath?

4. How did you get here, and what are you meant to learn from this?

5. What is the role of forgiveness in healing?

6. Trust in your ability to create your heart's desire.

7. Take action to create the life you really want.

8. Slow down: examine and honor all of your involvements.

9. Take risks, try new things . . . and pay attention to how you feel.

10. Let your female friends help you.

11. Learn what men have to offer and what they cannot do for you.

12. Invite joy, pleasure, and passion into your life.

13. Stay present to the gift of the moment.

14. Celebrate your newfound freedom, fulfillment, and fabulous good fortune.

You've just read through the list of 14 key questions or lessons. As you explore each of them during our time together, keep in mind that there's a personal right path for you to heal your life. As you go through this book, you'll read many examples and suggestions. I urge you to be gentle with yourself. Please don't compare yourself to others or judge your own process. Let yourself learn from each story and point. But keep in mind that you (like all of us) feel, see, and grow in your own time and in your own blessedly unique way.

You may find that some of the lessons really touch you where you most need to be healed, while others don't resonate for you right now. That's fine! Trust that you'll get just what you need when you need it. Work on the lessons as the fancy strikes you. Healing is a self-paced process!

Writing helps! You may benefit from making notes in the margins of this book or by keeping a journal to jot down your feelings, thoughts, and ideas as you go along. Be creative! Draw, paint, or find other ways to make these lessons your own. I know they can help you heal your life. And I'm *sure* you'll be successful!

Chapter 1

WHAT IS BETRAYAL, HOW DOES IT FEEL, AND WHERE CAN IT TAKE YOU?

What Is Betrayal?

Betrayal is a breach of trust. What you counted on to be true is false. You were living a lie. When you've been betrayed by your beloved, spouse, or life partner, your world shatters. The person you thought you could believe in has deceived you. You're alone. You've been abandoned. You're at risk. The vows and commitments you made to one another become meaningless. You don't know who you are anymore or who that other person really is. Your whole notion of your life history is challenged. What was real, and what was not?

One of the most common and devastating forms of betrayal involves extra-relational intimacy of an emotional and/or physical nature. By conservative estimates, 40 percent of women and 60 percent of men will have an affair at some point. When you've been betrayed in this way, your life partner has chosen to share himself with someone else. He has lied to you about his whereabouts and activities. He has led you to believe one thing when in reality the truth was something totally, and devastatingly, different.

You may find out about the betrayal when your partner tells you the truth; or you may trip over evidence, be told by someone else, or discover your partner in the act of deception. But no matter how the reality begins to come to you, it will rock you to your very core. In fact, betrayal may well be the cruelest and most painful relationship challenge you'll ever face. It's devastating. And it has the potential to undermine and destroy you forever . . . *if you let it!* Here's an example of how betrayal can derail a life.

When she began seeing me for counseling, Pam was a beautiful, creative, vibrant, successful 32-year-old professional. She came to me two years after her divorce, because she was still depressed and highly self-critical. She was pining for her ex-husband. This was a man who had told her during their honeymoon that he wasn't sure he loved her, and within nine months of marriage had informed her that he wanted a divorce. Additionally, she learned that during their marriage, he had been having an affair with the woman he was about to marry.

Two years later, Pam still missed her ex-husband and resented his happiness. She felt personally robbed of the possibility of a future as a wife and mother. She saw no chance of any joy for herself down the line.

I wondered about the history of Pam's relationship with her ex-husband. How had she come to choose him? And why was she idealizing such a dishonest and hurtful man? I was extremely concerned about how much power she was giving her ex to write the script for her future, and I was grateful she'd come to me to learn how to heal her own life in the aftermath of such devastation.

Betrayal feels awful . . . and it brings forth many different emotions. Pam's story illustrates a few of them.

Let's look at some of the common reactions, questions, and experiences that arise in response to betrayal. While we can't cover everything, you'll probably see yourself in many of these descriptions and stories. Even so, some of what you've lived may be missing from this short list. No matter what you've been through, though, you're not alone. Others have been there, too!

How Does Betrayal Feel, and Where Can It Take You?

It can't be true.

Often the first reaction people have upon discovering they've been betrayed is shock, denial, or minimization of the full reality of what they've learned. Weird as it may seem, this reaction makes a lot of sense. Our survival as a species depends on our maintaining a certain amount of healthy denial. We can't walk around focusing on all the frightening and negative things that could happen to us in life or we'd never get out of bed in the morning, cross the street, or turn on our car ignitions! Some denial or minimization of risk is necessary for healthy functioning. Without it, we'd never let our children out of sight, invest our money in the stock market, or change jobs.

It's healthy to take in negative news with a grain, or even a saltshaker full, of doubt. *Maybe it's not true, or perhaps it's not as bad as all that,* we tell ourselves. *Let's not get too far ahead of ourselves . . . let's calm down.* The worse the news is—or the more threatening or devastating it has the potential to be— the more likely we are to push it down, or even out.

So, for example, after Jenny discovered that her husband, Jack, had been engaging in homosexual banter with men on the Internet, one night she woke from sleep with a start. All of a sudden, she realized that he may have been involved in sexual activities with those men he was talking to. When, to her horror, she learned that he *had* in fact participated in many illicit homosexual trysts, it took her a few days to register the extent of the health risks to which she had been exposed and the necessity of getting herself "checked out" for a gamut of STDs. (Thankfully, she was found to be clear of all diseases. She is currently divorced and well on her way to realizing her heart's desire.)

Here's another example. I call it the *phone call from hell.* Alice answered the phone. John was on the line. He introduced himself and told Alice that he was calling to tell her that Dan, her husband, had been having an affair with his wife. She hung up on John and totally pushed the call out of her mind for several days. She *forgot* it! Why? She couldn't even contemplate the possibility of infidelity. When, several weeks later, the memory reemerged, she confronted her husband. To his credit, Dan admitted to her that John was speaking the truth. (Not all partners will come clean, not at first . . . or at all.)

Because Dan was anxious to salvage his marriage, he pushed for marital counseling. He and Alice became my patients, and both took on the reality of their issues and relationship challenges. Each spent some separate time in a rehabilitation program—Dan for sexual addiction and Alice for codependency. They went through a long marital separation as well. After much individual therapy and couples counseling, they eventually reconciled. Years of work led to a stable and satisfying marriage.

As the tales of Jenny and Alice illustrate, denial and minimization are often the first responses people have to being betrayed. And the experience comes in waves and stages. Those defenses will arise over and over again to protect you. You'll tell yourself: *It's real . . . it's not real. Maybe this part is true . . . but that part can't be . . . maybe I'm blowing it out of proportion. . . .*

You've probably gone back and forth already. Remember that you can only let in and process so much at a time. Be patient with yourself as you block out and progressively allow yourself to register more and more of what is . . . and don't beat yourself up as you navigate through the process. Moving back and forth is inevitable in order to keep yourself sane and functional.

"How Could You Have?"

Another response to betrayal that also comes in waves is horror, anger, and disbelief. "How could you possibly have done that?" we may rage. "Who do you think you are, anyway? . . . How dare you! . . . Don't you care about me, our children, or your reputation? You are a horrid beast. I hate you!"

In raging, questioning, and even name-calling, we're trying to make sense of the unfathomable. Our world *can't* be exploding. How dare anyone devastate us so much?! We need safety. We want to annihilate the annihilator. We need to be able to trust in the stability of our worlds and in the reliability of our intimates. When those closest to us threaten our very existence, we respond with shock and rage. It's self-protective and inevitable. We need to take control, take charge, and take action. It's empowering and deeply healing. So let it rip . . . as long as it doesn't go on too long, and no one gets physically injured in the process. Let's look at an example together.

When Hannah discovered that her live-in lover, Ron, was sleeping with her best friend, she pulled out each one of his dresser drawers and dumped the contents onto their living-room floor. She then took every suit, shirt, and pair of pants of Ron's in the closet and threw them in a heap on the kitchen floor.

In describing the scene to me, Hannah said that hurling one item of her boyfriend's wardrobe after another felt empowering and healing. "I kept imagining that I was throwing the clothes at him," she said. "It felt really good!" And when every stitch of clothing was out of the bedroom, she wrote a note and placed it atop one of the clothing piles. It said: "I hate you. Get out and stay out. I never want to see you again."

When Ron came home several hours later, with flowers and an apology card, she felt ready to hear what he had to say. Having felt and enacted her anger, she was able to be receptive to his remorse . . . and to her pain. It enabled her to move to another level of processing.

In order to move forward in healing, we need to make space for our shock, horror, and anger—and even full-on rage. It's human nature to experience all of those feelings. For some of us, they'll emerge right away; for others of us, they may remain quiescent for a long time. While I described an active, intense show of anger in Hannah's tale, some of us tend instead to become steely cold and put up a huge wall when we're betrayed. We may tie our lovers' clothes up in a bag and leave it on the bed with the implied message: *take your stuff and get out.* But we won't say anything. We might even go out and party with our friends to distract ourselves. We'll do what we need to do to ensure that we don't have to deal with our betrayers in person.

Anger can be scary . . . and some of us will retreat in fear and self-blame rather than feeling it toward those who hurt us. We may not even be aware of our anger at all. Fearfulness of this emotion is especially prominent if we've been abused in childhood. And we may not recognize the existence or extent of our childhood abuse experiences until our betrayers are well out of our lives.

You experience anger differently from the next person. Be gentle with yourself as you navigate the waves of shock, disbelief, and anger. Know that your feelings will emerge as they're meant to. Honor them as they come up . . . learn from them. Your healing is dependent on this. There's no need to control them—just let them be, without judgment.

"What Did You Do? Where? When? Why?"

We need information to understand and make sense of our betrayal:

- Who knows about the betrayal?
- Who was involved?
- Who will stand by us?
- Has our main support become our greatest threat?
- What does this mean?

In asking these questions, we're trying to figure out how much of our sense of reality, our take on past experiences, can be trusted. What is actually *real?* We need to feel in control. How broken is our world? Is it like Humpty Dumpty—can it ever be put back together again? Do we even want to *try?* What risks do we face? What will our future be?

Renée and her husband had dealt with, and worked through, an episode of infidelity early in their marriage. He had ended the affair and vowed not to stray again. So when Renée discovered that her husband of 15 years was back in touch with the woman he had been sexually involved with, she was devastated. She'd been happy in her marriage for 12 years. She was a retired executive without a separate income, and she'd been through a painful divorce in her past. Her husband was her family. She had no children; and her only sibling, a sister, lived in a foreign country.

Renée desperately needed to know what she could trust, and she was extremely fearful of what leaving the marriage would mean for her ability to provide for herself. She couldn't decide what to do—stay or go? She sought counseling to make sense of her experience and chart the best future course for herself.

For many of us, we need to know details to make sense of our pasts, presents, and futures. We require a certain amount of information to heal our lives after betrayal. And our need may change over time.

But I want to introduce a caveat here: any one of us can get so caught up in learning and sleuthing out the details of our betrayal experience that we lose track of our own reactions, self-care, and growth process. I'll share more about this concept in the next chapter, but it can't be emphasized enough.

We women are experts at shifting our attention onto others and away from ourselves and our own needs and challenges. We're self-sacrificing, caring, loving, other-oriented beings. We make great mothers, wives, friends, and volunteers. And we often treat our pets, plants, and neighbors better than we do ourselves. We're used to ignoring our own joys, hurts, and pains and focusing on those of others.

I urge you to learn *only* as much as you *need to know* about your betrayal experience in order to heal your life. Be careful of what you ask for . . . you may get more information than you need, or even want to have. Remember—healing is about, and for, *you!*

What's Wrong with Me? Am I Not Enough?

All too often we respond to being betrayed by doubting ourselves and our own value. We wonder how desirable we are. We may even begin to believe that we're not enough—thin enough, attractive enough, smart enough, giving enough, easygoing enough, sexy enough, loving enough. We quickly and readily take on the responsibility for our partners' choices to look elsewhere for sex or intimacy. We rush to blame ourselves for someone else's actions.

We women are bombarded by the media with constant messages that we're not good enough. And given our feminine natures—our relational, harmony-seeking orientation— we're apt to take on the blame for others' decisions and actions. Furthermore, our betrayers often fuel our self-critical mentality by finding fault with us and criticizing us for all sorts of perceived shortcomings.

Know now and hear me, loud and clear: You are *not* responsible for your partner's choices and actions. *You are fabulous, loving, and <u>enough.</u>* You definitely have things to learn about how you got to this point in your life and where you're meant to go from here. And you *will* learn them! But you're not to blame for this crisis in your world. You're more than good enough! And there is *nothing* wrong with you!

I'm Not Surprised—I <u>Knew</u> Something Was Going On

In the midst of the horror of discovering they've been betrayed, some women feel validated and even relieved. Even though their worlds are falling apart, they're developing clarity. They've been experiencing the fallout of betrayal—the energetic results of their partners' secret lives. Yet they haven't known how to respond to their experiences. They've been misled and lied to, and maybe even criticized for the suspicions and concerns they've raised. They've known—without *totally* knowing—that their partners were betraying them.

Cassandra's story is a case in point:

> "I finally found the evidence I knew was there," my patient told me during our first visit. Her volunteer-firefighter husband had inadvertently left his computer on when he had to rush out of the house for a fire call one morning. When she approached his desk to retrieve his empty coffee cup and half-eaten muffin, her jaw dropped: there, displayed on his computer screen, were a series of images of children engaged in sexual activities with adult partners. With a few clicks of the mouse, Cassandra discovered a huge file of child pornography, and evidence that her husband was part of a pornography ring.
>
> Deeply disturbed, but relieved to have found validation for her sense of foreboding and an explanation for her husband's erratic behavior, Cassandra came to see me for advice and guidance. "What do I do with all this information?" she wanted to know. "And where do I go from here? Is it even safe for me to confront him? Whom should I tell? I have to say, weird as it seems, I'm relieved to discover that I'm not crazy. Maybe this

came now to tell me that my marriage is over. I've been thinking that I need to get out for a long time. But he kept telling me I was imagining things. After a while, I stopped knowing what to trust! I lost touch with myself. Thank God for the clarity I'm getting now."

Although I was immediately deeply concerned when I heard Cassandra's revelation about her husband's activities, my role was to encourage her to take action and report what he was doing to the proper authorities at an appropriate time in her own healing process—something she was finally able to do.

In Cassandra's case, the validation of her gut sense, and the specific evidence she found, was helpful in enabling her to move on. But you can also be validated by what you learn and still have the desire to try to heal your partnership. Relief can come in the truth being revealed . . . no matter where you ultimately choose to take it.

Now What? Where Do I Go from Here?

When our worlds explode, it's inevitable that we worry about what will come next. From our positions of panic, we ask, *Now what? Where do I go from here?* Often my patients say, "I don't know what to do."

When I learned of my husband's infidelity and scary behavior, I felt as if I'd been hit in the gut with a bowling ball. I sat at my desk in shock, horror, disbelief, and relief all at once. I had no idea what to do . . . and I knew exactly what I needed: *support.* I needed to talk. I needed validation. I needed to not feel so alone!

I called a dear friend, Shirley, who, 22 years before, had been betrayed in a similarly humiliating manner by her first husband. She was the perfect one to call. Her loving encouragement and moral indignation were just what I needed to experience at that moment in time. After about half an hour on the phone with Shirley, I felt better; I was connected, buoyed, and comforted. *I'm not alone in this,* I thought. *Many others have been through similar challenges, have survived, and even have <u>thrived.</u> I'll get through this, too, with the help of my friends.* And so I did . . . as have many others.

The road to healing your life after betrayal is through love, guidance, and hope. You may not know "what to do" in a big way for a long time. But, day by day, you will! Reach out to your friends, trusted relatives, colleagues, therapist, mentors, religious leaders, and any other spiritual resources that speak to you. You'll gain clarity, love, and support.

And you have a choice about how to proceed. While you can't control the winds, you can surely choose how you respond to them. You direct your sails! In the next chapter, you'll learn the lesson of choice. Do you grow or shrink, learn or blame, or leave or stay? You actively choose your future . . . one minute at a time. And you absolutely can create the world of your dreams. Are you ready? Let's go!

Chapter 2

YOU HAVE A CHOICE: DO YOU SEIZE YOUR POWER OR BECOME THE VICTIM?

*L*ife is all about choice. You've heard that before. You know these expressions: *Life is what you make of it. You reap what you sow. You get what you expect to receive. You are the captain of your own ship. Life is a self-fulfilling prophecy.* And maybe even, *You've made your bed; now you must lie in it.*

While there is some truth to all of those popular sayings, I want you to be cautious and gentle with yourself in how you interpret them.

Yes, we all have free choice. And every second, each of us must decide how we want to look at and respond to the myriad challenges and opportunities that come our way. We can choose to see the cup as half-full or half-empty. We do have some control. However, while we can control our responses *most* of the time, we surely can't control anyone else's. And we're definitely not responsible for the thoughts, words, ideas, and behavior of other people.

What that means is that when your world explodes in betrayal, you may lose control of your emotions and actions for a while. You can't help but be thrown into denial, despair, hopelessness, rage, and blame. And in the process of coping with the massive challenges facing you, you may feel, say, and do things that you would never choose to in your right mind. Rest assured that you're not alone if, temporarily, you become a person you don't recognize or wouldn't even want to know.

You may find yourself bad-mouthing your partner in ways that later disturb you, and you might wish him harm. You may feel the need to be right, heard, understood, and validated. You could even desire or seek revenge. In other words, you may find you're not yourself for a very long time.

This chapter is about how you choose to deal with your betrayal experience in an overarching and ongoing way. It's about the chance you have to turn what feels like a horrible disaster into a wonderful opportunity. You may not feel, or even see, the opportunity or gift in every moment. But the more you remember and remind yourself that there's a blessing in every curse, an upside to every downturn, a fresh possibility in every setback, and a future in every demise . . . the easier it will be for you to heal your life when your world explodes. Let's look at an example of what I mean. I'll use my own story.

When my world exploded in betrayal, I was supposed to be starting my third book. I had a contract with my wonderful publisher, Hay House, and was supposed to deliver *Loving the Good-Enough Life* five months from that fateful day.

I'm sure that you, having been there, can understand that I was in no position to write that book—or *any* book for that matter. It was all I could do to keep putting one foot in front of the other. I had, for all intents and purposes, just become a single parent of four children. Beyond that, as a doctor with a part-time clinical practice, I had patients to care for and numerous other professional activities to maintain.

So I called my fabulous editor at Hay House, Jill Kramer, and told her that I needed an extension on my book-delivery date. When I explained what I was dealing with, Jill was appropriately horrified, and deeply concerned about me.

"Oh my God! . . . Are you going to be okay?" she asked. "Of course, take as much time as you need," she added. "How can we help you?"

If you've read any of my previous books or kits, you know how optimistic, positive, and upbeat I am. You know my MO: "Where there's a will, there's a way." It's not what life throws at us that counts, but how we choose to handle it. I've helped many people heal their lives by employing, and maintaining, that perspective.

But why am I going on about my beliefs and my prior books right now? Well, so you'll understand the lesson of this vignette, of course. As soon as Jill conveyed her concern, I responded: "I'm going through hell right now. But, thank God, I believe everything I write. There's a reason for this. I'm going to be okay. In fact, I'm going to be better off in the end."

I made a decision to choose the healing path. Even though I was feeling awful, I chose to be hopeful and to see the opportunity in the crisis. I decided to make my life better than it had been before. As time went on, I kept reminding myself to choose hope and empowerment. I didn't do a perfect job. But when I sat down to talk to my children, I echoed the positive sentiment: "You don't need to worry. We're all going through a very difficult time—and it may go on for many months—but we're going to be fine in the end. We're all safe. We have our health. We have each other. We love one another. You don't deserve this, and I'm sorry you have to deal with this pain. Luckily, I have enough money to take care of us. And someday, our life will be better than it was before."

When my world exploded, I was overwhelmed and afraid. I suffered and struggled a lot. But all the while, I chose to focus on the positive—to grasp the gift, to articulate it, and to make it real. I've helped many others do the same thing. And if my patients and I can heal our lives in that way, so can you.

To Blame or to Learn

When your world explodes, you get rocked to your very core. Much of what made sense before becomes meaningless. It's "normal" to cast about looking for someone to blame, someone to hold responsible for throwing you into this pit of despair, this tailspin, this agony. And it's easy to *find* such a someone. Betrayal involves dishonest, unethical, hurtful actions, so you may feel compelled to blame your partner. You might find it easier to blame those with whom your partner engaged. Or you may be most comfortable blaming yourself!

We have a self-protective tendency to make someone the culprit when we've been hurt. It helps us explain what is otherwise unfathomable. It's crucial to allow ourselves to feel anger and moral indignation when we've been misused. It's healthy to search for causes and explanations and to try to figure out who is responsible for what has occurred. *But . . . we need to beware of blame.* We need to guard against our tendency to make the explosion of emotion *all* about faultfinding, because it interferes with healing our lives when our worlds shatter.

The more we blame ourselves or others for our misfortune, the more powerless we become. We turn into victims. We give up our free will, our gift to choose, and our opportunity to learn.

Let's look at an example. Think back to Pam's story in Chapter 1. Remember her? She had been divorced for two years, and she came to me because she still believed that her ex-husband had destroyed her potential for a joyous future. He was to blame, and *she* was the loser. She saw no good options for herself.

You won't be surprised to learn that I urged Pam to stop focusing on him. When she began her work with me, she was actively involved in training to be a yoga teacher. Since she was immersed in a practice whose focus was on the here-and-now without judgment, I urged her to begin applying the teachings of that yogic tradition to her present-day life challenges.

"Focusing on what was done to you in the past won't help you in the present," I told her. "What's done is done. It's finished, over, complete. You surely have something to learn from it. I wonder what got you into that bad marriage in the first place? Why do you continue to idealize him? To learn about yourself is to reclaim *your* power, but making it about him does the opposite."

Pam and I worked at letting go and shifting the focus. As she began to release blame, my patient could begin creating the life *she* really wanted! To that end, she made a career change, a geographic move, and a new circle of friends. And I'm thrilled to be able to tell you that she's happier today than she has been for years. She's currently dating men who are more available, appropriate, and suitable for her than her ex-husband ever was . . . and I'm sure she'll find a soul mate! Why do I say that? Because a husband and children complete the picture of her heart's desire, and she's actively doing what she needs to do to get there.

You see, blame holds us hostage. It says: "I am struggling, in pain, and so on because of what was done to me. There is nothing I can do about it. I was a passive bystander. I am the victim. I played no part in what occurred . . . and I can't do anything to change it." It keeps us stuck, angry, and miserable.

Growth requires us to banish blame and seize the opportunity to learn. We must determine who is responsible for what, and which pieces we need to own and shift in order to move forward.

There's a big difference between *blaming* and holding people responsible for their actions. Healing your life when you've been betrayed requires you to assign responsibility, ownership, and control where it belongs. If you don't do that, you'll never learn from your experience. You won't see your mistakes or discover what you need to do to better care for yourself going forward.

There are reasons you chose, and stayed with, the person who ultimately betrayed you. Because of your nature and history, you were drawn to pieces of his character. And for similar reasons, you played your part in that ongoing dynamic that ultimately led you to this monumental time in your life. Your healing work involves figuring out what you unwittingly chose to do, and why.

I'll use my own story as an example again. You'll see how I replayed a childhood dynamic in choosing and staying with my ex-husband.

One of the roles I played growing up was that of caretaker to my clinically depressed mother. Back then, I didn't know she was suffering from a condition that had an actual name. And given who she was, she refused to admit that there was a problem or seek treatment of any sort. Yet in a controlling and guilt-provoking way, she made it clear to me, as the oldest of three children and the only daughter, that I was to parent her and my younger brothers. She would retreat to her bedroom every evening and refuse to engage. My dad was working most nights, and I was expected to care for my siblings. I wasn't to complain or share my perspective. If I got upset, she told me I was too emotional. I learned to suck it up and ignore my feelings. I became an "over-parentified," self-sacrificing child by the time I was ten years old. (I don't blame her today—she was too ill to know better. But I do hold her responsible for her role.)

Fast-forward to my first year of medical school. I met a man who was clearly interested in me. And if you've read my first book, *There's Always Help; There's Always Hope,* you know that I was miserable at that time. I was very depressed about what medical training was turning out to be. So, when that man, a year ahead of me in school, began talking about his own distress and depression during his first year, I connected with him.

As soon as he began to share his personal struggles and family-of-origin challenges, I got hooked. I stepped into a familiar role. I became the listener, caretaker, supporter, and problem solver. As you may recall from my previous book and/or the Introduction to this one, I quickly married that man when my mother urged me to do so.

In many ways, I played the caretaker and problem solver throughout the course of my marriage. As things got worse, I tried harder to make them better. And I was very unhappy. Today, I know that I tried way too hard, and for far too long! There was no way my efforts were going to bear fruit. *He* wasn't going to change, and *I* was never going to be happy with him. But it took the implosion of my marriage for me to get that lesson loud and clear. And I'm very grateful for that gift of "implosion." Without it, it would have taken me longer to get out. I wouldn't yet be as happy as I am today.

Now, not all betrayals are meant to teach you to get out. (We'll explore that issue later in this chapter.) But all offer you a choice: You have the opportunity to seize your power or become the victim. You have the choice to learn or to blame. You can grow or shrink. You may soul-search . . . or focus on others. You have the opportunity to create your heart's desire. You're in charge, and only you can choose just who *you* want to be.

Just Who Will You Be?

Maria Shriver wrote a wonderful little book with the title *Just Who Will You Be?* It's actually the speech she gave at her nephew's high-school graduation and her thoughts before and after giving it. She asks a *great* question.

At times of calm and joy in our lives, at times of small setbacks, and at times of major personal challenge, we have the opportunity and responsibility to ask ourselves that same question. *Just who will I be?* Not *What will I do?* or *Where will I live?* or *What job titles will I acquire?* but just . . . *Who will I be?* In other words . . .

- *What do I believe?*
- *What kind of person do I want to be?*
- *What is really important to me?*
- *What are my goals, hopes, dreams, and desires; and have they changed?*
- *Does what served me in the past meet my needs today?*
- *What makes my heart sing?*
- *What kind of choices do I want to make?*
- *What values and beliefs do I hold and want to live by?*
- *And when I face great devastation in my life, what matters most to me?*

Healing your life when your world explodes is really all about deciding just who you will be. Will you choose joy or pain, growth or blame, today or yesterday, your heart's desire or someone else's script? You needn't be a victim. Remember that you got yourself to this point. And you can surely move forward to bigger and better things. Will you honor your inner wisdom and choose to become your best self?

When my life exploded, I took a serious personal inventory. I thought long and hard about what was most important to me and how much the life I'd created reflected my desires. How did I get to where I was, and what did I want to change?

I realized that what mattered most to me was missing from my life. My dearest wish was a soul mate: an honest, principled, funny, loving, giving, passionate, intelligent, self-assured, sexy, open-minded, self-supporting, healthy, loyal, and spiritual man. I wanted a partner who had been married in the past, and who had been faithful to his wife. I wanted to be with a man who had a child or children, as well as a good relationship with them. I wanted to be with someone who would see and love me, who shared my worldview and family values, and whose company I would enjoy.

I realized that I had always wanted *that* type of soul mate. But I was looking for love in the wrong place. My ex-husband was never that kind of person, and he wasn't *going* to be. In the specific actions and details of the betrayal, I was shown just how wrong my choice had been. So, what did I do? I chose to welcome the crisis . . . and let go of my old role. I decided to put my energies into finding a right fit, instead of attempting to fit a round peg into a square hole.

Perhaps you've read the fabulous best-selling book *Eat, Pray, Love*. It's a memoir by Elizabeth Gilbert. While it's not about betrayal, it *is* about the author's decision to leave a marriage, and her subsequent growth. If you haven't read it, you might want to do so. At the beginning of the book, Gilbert realizes that *she never really wanted the life she chose.*

I think the book has such appeal because this tale resonates for many of us. In *Eat, Pray, Love,* Gilbert chronicles her odyssey to find herself. She shares her journey to wholeness and joy. She describes, in beautiful and funny prose, the work she had to do to heal. She had to learn how to let go. She needed to discover her spiritual place in the universe. Those tasks had to be accomplished before she could find a love that was right for her. She finds herself quite surprised by what she learns. What ultimately brings her joy isn't what she ever expected she'd want or choose!

Your betrayal experience offers *you* the opportunity to find yourself as well. And you, too, may be pleasantly surprised by where it takes you. I surely have been. Gilbert was. Many of my patients have been. Let yourself be open to surprise and wonder. Miracles happen! Ask yourself: *What do I most want? Have I been living it? What needs to change? . . . Just who will I be?*

To Leave or to Stay?

One of the biggest questions you may be confronting is whether to leave your relationship or stay in it. Betrayal causes tremendous pain and damage to any relationship; and your feelings about how you want to proceed may evolve as you learn more about your partner's behavior, how honest he is, how much he owns his part, whether he's truly sorry, and whether he's committed to making it right by working to heal your relationship. You may be wondering if the damage is so severe that it ought to break the two of you up. Perhaps you're consumed by whether you can afford to leave. Do you believe you need to stay because you have children together? (I thought I did, for a long time! Many of my patients have, too.) Are you concerned that you won't be able to survive the pain if you do choose to stay . . . or if you choose to leave?

My clinical work and personal life experience have taught me that there is a right answer for each person—but no *universal* right answer. In your heart of hearts, in your gut, you'll know what's best for you to do. You might realize it right away. It may take you a while to get that clarity. And, of course, having children with the partner who has betrayed you makes it harder to decide to leave.

While you, and only you, can decide what's best for *you*, I'd like to share some principles and guidelines with you to help you answer the stay-versus-go question for yourself. If these ideas are inadequate to get you off the fence, I suggest you pick up a copy of the book *Too Good to Leave, Too Bad to Stay,* by Mira Kirshenbaum, and work through the diagnostic questions designed to help you decide whether to stay in or get out of your relationship. It's a fabulous book! Some of the ideas that you'll be reading in this section can be found in it and are developed in more detail there. Kirshenbaum provides examples and great guidance, too!

Here are some crucial guidelines:

1. If you've never really been happy in the relationship, it's unreasonable to think that you will be in the future. If it's never worked, it can't be fixed. And you deserve more. Give yourself that gift.

2. Having children together is *not* a good reason to stay in a bad relationship. Doing so will teach *them* to sacrifice joy and self-actualization in the same way. Is that the example you want to provide? No studies have ever compared the impact on kids of parents staying together in terrible relationships versus parents in that same situation divorcing. My clinical experience, and that of many others,

THE GIFT OF BETRAYAL

is that being raised in a toxic environment is destructive to children. If you stay when it's really too bad for you to do so, your children will learn to do the same thing. Trust that following your heart and your gut will serve you—and those you love—the best.

3. **If your partner won't come clean and commit to ending the offending behaviors, if he justifies his actions and criticizes you, or if he doesn't demonstrate true remorse and a desire to heal your pain, the relationship won't work.** Many studies have shown this. Healing betrayal in marriage is a painful and arduous process when there *is* willingness and a desire to try to do so on both sides. If the perpetrator isn't honest, sorry, empathetic, and engaged in that process, it's doomed to failure. Don't beat a dead horse.

4. **If you can no longer respect your partner, there is no way you can have a satisfying relationship with him.** I think this one can stand without further elucidation. We can't be partners if we don't respect one another.

5. **If the crime is so terrible that *anyone* would have trouble forgiving and forgetting it, it's unlikely *you* will be able to do so.** You're only human. Don't hold yourself to a standard no one can live up to.

6. **If your partner wants out, it's a blessing in disguise— no relationship with an unwilling, unengaged person can serve you.** Remember that you can control you, and only you, so you can't make a relationship work with someone who doesn't want a future with you. And his betrayal was an outgrowth of his lack of investment. It's wonderful to be released from a union that can't possibly serve you. Let yourself see this as a release from bondage. It's a blessing!

7. If your heart isn't invested in fixing it, your relation-ship is already over. Grasp the gift and get the heck out! You're allowed to be finished! Your betrayal may have been the last straw for you in a problematic relationship. Or it may have served to devastate too much of what you hold dear for you to make it work.

8. If you're not ready to leave the relationship, it's not yet time for you to go, with one exception (see Guideline 9 below). Many people have to visit their pain and dissatisfaction from multiple angles, and for a long time, before they decide to leave what doesn't work . . . or stay because it becomes *workable*. More often than not, those who come to me for treatment after betrayal are in my office because they need help getting out . . . and it can take them as little as a few months—and as long as several years—to develop clarity and be ready to leave. Be open to therapy or counseling if you feel stuck here. Many women need support to get out.

9. If your partner has physically abused you on more than one occasion, you *must* leave! Your well-being is on the line. This is a life-and-death issue.

10. If you're involved with a sociopath, your relation-ship will get worse. The longer you stay in it, the more you stand to lose. Cut your losses and move on! You'll learn more about this guideline in Chapter 3.

11. It takes two to tango—healing the relationship requires both of you to engage fully. If you have an inner desire to give it a try, and so does he, it's worth doing. This is probably obvious. But keep in mind that if *your* desire . . . or *his* willingness . . . changes, it's time to reevaluate your decision.

12. What feels right at first may well change. It can be hard to let go of your hopes, prayers, and dreams when they've been shattered. You may cling to a sinking ship. Conversely, you might find that it's easier to jump ship when you've been betrayed than hang around long enough to figure out if the vessel is actually seaworthy after all.

Be patient with yourself. Allow yourself to follow your heart, and to change your mind as often as need be in the process. Think about these questions:

- *What is my pattern?*
- *Do I try too hard to make the unworkable work; or do I tend to go whenever "the going gets tough"?*
- *How might I be enacting my ongoing dynamic now?*
- *Do I need help to figure out where I stand?*

Please be open to help and surprise! Ultimately, your inner wisdom will be your guide, and you *will* figure out the right answer for you!

Staying In

If you choose to stay in, at least for the time being, what will it be like? Well, the best answer I can give you is . . . *it will be hell for a long time*. Healing betrayal is a lengthy and very difficult process. Many others have traveled that road. It surely *can* be done. You and your partner can emerge from the experience stronger and more deeply committed to one another. You can find a future together, if that's your heart's desire.

But it will take a long time to get there, and you'll jointly need to work through a lot of issues. Most important, you'll need to learn how to build a partnership rooted in honesty and mutual respect. You must confront issues of trust, reliability, self-esteem, doubt, guilt, shame, and blame . . . along with a deep pain. You'll probably each need a lot of individual support and will—most likely—require some marital counseling as well.

If staying in feels at all right to you, I suggest you pick up a copy of Peggy Vaughan's book *The Monogamy Myth: A Personal Handbook for Recovering from Affairs*. The author is one of the leading experts on the topic of infidelity, having worked and written in this field for almost 30 years. She, too, went through her own experience of betrayal when her husband of 11 years began having affairs that lasted 7 years. She shares a path to healing that may help you follow your heart to wholeness. While she chose to stay and was able to work it out with her husband, she recognizes and teaches that there's a right personal answer for each individual. I highly recommend her work.

Leaving

If you choose to leave, what will it be like? In some ways, it will be just like staying in. It may be hell for a long time . . . even if, on many levels, it feels immediately better.

Getting out is tough. A permanent breakup is always difficult . . . and sometimes excruciating. Dreams die. Futures collapse. Our past loves may even become our greatest adversaries. When the relationship involved marriage, the legal system steps in to help—and sometimes complicate what's already very difficult. If we have children together, custody and child-support issues can become torturous and feel never ending. Accusations may fly back and forth. Fear, hopelessness, and despair may knock regularly at our door and enter or settle into our souls.

But the wisdom of the expression *This, too, shall pass* can guide us through challenging times. On a particularly difficult day, one of my dearest friends said to me: "I don't know if this helps you, but when I get worried, I often remind myself that nothing is permanent." I found myself revisiting her words often when fear would strike me during the long year it took me to get through a contentious divorce and custody battle.

Nothing is forever. You *will* emerge out the other side; the sun will rise again. Spring and rebirth will come. There's always hope . . . and your future can surely be brighter than your past. *You will overcome.* Nothing is forever.

Most people who choose to leave need a ton of support, too. I urge you to get it. It will make a world of difference.

In Closing

As we end this chapter together, I want to reiterate its main point. *Although you've been betrayed, it's up to you to decide what happens next.* You have a choice: Do you seize your power or become the victim? Do you learn about yourself and grow . . . or blame and shrink? Do you stay, or do you leave? Do you see this challenge as an opportunity to create your heart's desire? Do you heal? *Just who will you be?*

You have a choice. And healing your life when your world explodes requires you to seize the gift and grow. I urge you to give yourself that future!

Chapter 3

COULD YOU HAVE BEEN MARRIED TO (OR INVOLVED WITH) A SOCIOPATH?

*C*ould you be married to (or involved with) a sociopath? This chapter contains a lesson that ought to be highlighted in bold colors. It stands alone for many of my patients as the "If only I had known" lesson. And *I've* only recently learned it.

When I was brainstorming ideas for this book with my editor, Jill Kramer, and told her that I would be including this question in *The Gift of Betrayal,* she wisely said, "You ought to devote a whole chapter to that topic!" The more I thought about her words, the clearer it became to me that she was right.

It turns out that as many as 1 in 25 ordinary individuals has no conscience and can inflict extreme pain on others without feeling sorry or guilty. Such people don't care at all about the effects of their actions on society, their friends and family, or even their own children. They feel no guilt or remorse whatsoever. And they don't look anything like you might expect. They are *everywhere.* You could even be married to one!

During my psychiatry residency training, I was taught about sociopathy. But what I learned back then as dogma was totally wrong. Sociopathy was presented as synonymous with psychopathology. Sociopaths were hard-core criminals, mass murderers—obvious monsters. Sociopathy was relatively uncommon, and people with this diagnosis would rarely be our patients because they wouldn't stay long in treatment. They weren't troubled enough by anything to engage. Since they didn't feel emotional pain, guilt, or remorse, they wouldn't spend much time in the company of psychiatrists. Unless we were planning to go into forensic (legal) work, we didn't need to know much about this character problem!

Nothing could have been further from the truth. Today, I know that studies in psychology (cited in the book *The Sociopath Next Door,* which is discussed below) suggest that 1 in 25 individuals is a sociopath. Many of them are people you might least suspect of lacking conscience. They are teachers, doctors, leaders, dog walkers, and parents. They look just like you and me. And many of them have been my patients. They suffer from addictions, depression, attention deficit disorder, and a host of other problems that the rest of us experience. They can talk a good line, and they can appear to be deeply caring. But in truth, sociopaths have no conscience and no real capacity for empathy or love. And because they're wolves in sheep's clothing, they can be very dangerous.

I've learned about the realities of sociopathy from my relatives, friends, patients, and nonpsychiatrist colleagues. When describing their experiences with their ex-spouses and lovers, they would tell me: "He was a sociopath," and go on to describe the egregious behaviors of their partners. Some of those "teachers" were grateful to have gotten out of their prior relationships with their lives! They'd been snowed by swindlers, petty criminals, abusers, and addicts. They'd been drawn in by the "pity" principle and spent years empathizing with, and trying to help, people who were actually using, abusing, and betraying them behind their backs.

Several of my friends and patients recommended a phenomenal book about sociopathy to me. You may have read it, but if you haven't, you might want to do so now. It's called

The Sociopath Next Door. In it, Martha Stout, Ph.D., teaches us how to recognize sociopathy and how to deal with sociopaths. She explains that they are driven by the "game" of life, the desire to win, and the need to dominate. They have no conscience, no moral compass, and no emotional attachment. They refuse to acknowledge responsibility for their decisions or for the outcomes of those decisions. They view themselves as victims in one situation after another. They're compulsive liars and are driven by their urge to destroy others. They will frequently target individuals with "strong" characteristics—in other words, the more empathetic, giving, and caring you are, the more likely you are to be the object of a sociopath's attack. Scary . . . isn't it?

I want you to think long and hard now. Could you be involved with a sociopath? Is your partner a liar? Does he seem to care about you only when it's convenient for him? Does he frighten you? Create frequent problems that you have to solve? Appeal to your pity? Attack you? Blame you for the errors he makes and the crises he creates? Do you have, or have you ever had, any of the following series of horrifying thoughts:

- *I don't know who you are.*

- *How could you possibly have done such an appalling thing?*

- *You would sell me and your children down the river to suit yourself.*

- *How can you possibly live with yourself?*

- *You and I are on different planets—I can't fathom how you could have even thought to do that. And you actually <u>did</u> it!*

- *You don't care about anyone but yourself.*

If you identified with several of the questions and thoughts that you just read, you could well be (or have been) involved with a sociopath. You need to know if you are. Why do I say that? The reason is . . . *because sociopaths destroy people.*

The only way for you to heal your life, if a sociopath is part of it, is to get out of the relationship. You must avoid him as much as humanly possible—you must get as close as you can to total avoidance of that man. He is poison to your soul.

Here are some comments shared with me by women speaking about their sociopathic partners (several of whom were pillars of their communities!):

> *I married a man who turned out to be a gambler and a sociopath. I trusted him. I let him manage our finances because I hate doing that stuff. He stole all my money. And I had to buy my way out of my marriage. I am still afraid of him. I'll never be able to retire. I'll be paying him off for years.*

> *I've been going through a bitter divorce proceeding, and I just got copies of several prior court filings against my husband. He harassed a number of women. There are restraining orders against him from three of them. He is a stalker, a thief, and a drug addict. And he sees me as the problem! I'm so grateful to be getting out before he hurts me.*

> *I just found out that my husband has been stealing his employees' retirement money for three years and stole*

money from my elderly parents. They've been like parents to him. My mom called me to tell me what my husband did. A sheriff came to repossess my parents' home. That's how they discovered that my husband had been stealing their monthly payment checks for four months. Thank God they had the money to cover all those bills again. My husband has no remorse! And I don't even know who he is anymore. So, I've come to therapy for support. I'm planning to file for divorce.

My prior husband had an affair and then lied to all our friends about me. He made up all kinds of terrible stories. He wanted a divorce, and he didn't want to pay child support, so he used every technique he could think of to break me down until I stopped fighting for what was rightfully mine. He turned so many people against me. He hired an attorney known for legal harassment and used the legal system to attack me. I got to the point where I wanted to be done with him, no matter what the cost. When I assumed full custody and all expenses for our daughters, he finally signed the marital settlement agreement. That was 14 years ago. Some of our friends from that time still hate me and won't talk to me. I have no idea what he said to them.

Having read the preceding four statements made by women about their sociopathic partners, you may be wondering how anyone could get sucked in by such horrid-sounding men. And it's a valid question. Of course, much of the information those women shared with me came to them late in the game. But the question is still a good one.

It turns out that for those of us with a conscience, it's nearly impossible to imagine that someone else lacks such a fundamental characteristic. Conscience and caring are what make us human, so we tend to come up with a lot of excuses for unacceptable behavior. We explain it and understand it from our own perspectives. *That person must have had too much guilt or shame to do it differently,* we'll tell ourselves upon discovering the offending actions. And, of course, the sociopath will play on and appeal to our pity, our capacity and desire to empathize, and our instincts to forgive and try to help.

Smart sociopaths are very devious and convincing. For a long time they can look like the sensitive, wronged ones. Often they create the public persona of being caring, giving, or philanthropic individuals. This makes it especially hard for their spouses or partners to trust their own instincts or to feel supported in their distress. Partners of sociopaths will keep a ton of their pain and many of their experiences a secret. For these reasons, a nightmarish partnership with a sociopath can go on for a *very long* time.

Trauma/Betrayal Bonds

There is another extremely important reason why some women choose and stay with sociopathic partners. Their personal histories set them up to choose men who use and abuse them. And they stay in dangerous involvements because of a trauma bond, or what Patrick J. Carnes, Ph.D., calls the *betrayal bond* in his book of the same name. The betrayal bond is one forged by an exploitative relationship—a victim becomes attached to someone destructive to her and remains loyal to her partner even though he hurts, betrays, and exploits her. His betrayal actually intensifies the bond.

When in a betrayal bond, you experience a mind-numbing attachment to people who hurt you. You may try to explain their behavior, convert them into non-abusers, blame yourself, mistrust your own judgment, keep trying to fix the unfixable, and remain loyal to a person who is toxic and destructive to you. Being in a betrayal bond means that you're living a traumatic life. You're fearful, terrorized, and hyper-aroused. You never feel safe. You're forever on alert, waiting for the next crisis to arise. In this state, you lose touch with who you really are. Since you're continually fearing, hurting, and grieving, your joyful self goes underground. Your true self—what makes you tick—gets silenced. *You're no longer yourself!*

Because a betrayal or trauma bond can sneak up on you, it can be hard to recognize that you've stepped into a kind of insanity. You may not realize that you're living a craziness—doing the same thing over and over again and expecting different results. You may keep believing false promises, engaging in toxic fights that no one wins, trying to get your partner to see the truth about you, thinking you're stuck because he won't change, focusing on your partner's talents and overlooking his abuse of you, or moving closer to the one you fear. You may find yourself unable to detach from the person you no longer trust or even like! When your relationship is exploitative and scary like this and you can't get out, you're in a betrayal bond.

You may be wondering who would create, or step into, such a traumatic pit. And why would any intelligent, self-respecting individual *stay* there? If you're in, or have been in, a relationship like this, you may be beating yourself up for your "stupidity." Well, it turns out that your past history is your most powerful programmer in this regard.

Once you've been in a trauma bond—and often your first experience occurs during your childhood, years before you have choice—you're vulnerable to falling into similar patterns. Your history affects your neurochemistry. Your brain literally becomes programmed to re-create the trauma, so you'll be drawn to individuals who replay the relationship dynamic; and, over time, the power of the trauma bond will get greater. As a result, you may well pick, and stay with, more and more toxic individuals.

No one is immune to creating betrayal bonds. Anyone who is traumatized enough in a relationship can lose touch with herself and enter the insane vicious cycle of trauma bonding. Furthermore, the longer you stay in a betrayal bond or a relationship where your trust and safety are continually violated, the harder it can be to get out. This is one reason why some women keep going back to men who beat them up!

After my many years of clinical experience, I've come to the conclusion that trauma or betrayal bonds are *very* common. And I'm concerned that we don't talk about them enough when we visit issues of relationship and marriage viability. We don't talk enough about sociopathy, either. And, of course, you may well be in a trauma bond *with* a sociopath. These two things often go hand in hand. It's a terrible pit. But you *can* get out! The first step is to recognize where you are now.

So, let's regroup. Could you be married to or involved with a sociopath? If the answer is *yes,* you need to get out. If you're not sure of the answer by the end of this chapter, read *The Sociopath Next Door.* If you're in a trauma bond with a sociopath—or with anyone else, for that matter—you'll probably need some therapeutic help to get out. Seek whatever assistance you need in order to extricate yourself from the toxicity of traumatic involvements. There's no way you can heal your life if you're unsafe. So the first step is to get out of the repetitive abuse cycle. Then you can learn and grow.

I've seen many people reprogram their brains and lives after years of *horrendous* trauma. You can do it, too! We'll be exploring some of the techniques you can use to do that later in this book. Take heart! No matter your current circumstances, you can heal your life when your world explodes.

How Do I Deal with a Sociopath?

Now, what about dealing with sociopathy? In Martha Stout's book, she offers 13 rules for dealing with sociopaths in everyday life. I won't be covering them all, but I'd like to share several of her key points, as I understand them, and add a few of my own to the list. These concepts are fundamental to healing your life if a sociopath is part of your picture!

1. Suspend disbelief. *Believe* that some people have no conscience. That means that they have no moral compass and don't care about or really love anyone. The things that mean the most to you are actually meaningless to them. But they look like you and me . . . so, you could be married to one!

2. Trust your gut. Your instincts don't lie. Even if someone talks a good line or plays the part of a caring individual, he can be a wolf in sheep's clothing. If your relationship feels wrong or unsafe, it *is!*

3. Liars can't be trusted. If someone lies three times, he is a liar. Deceitfulness is the primary characteristic of people who lack conscience. Sociopaths are liars. You can't partner with a liar.

4. Pity has no place in a partnership. Beware of your tendency to pity too easily. This emotion is to be reserved for victims of disasters. It's not to be lavished on your spouse or life partner. If pity is a *cornerstone* of your relationship, you're very likely with a sociopath. Do whatever you must to get out!

5. You don't need him. You'll be just fine on your own. Sociopaths are highly manipulative and will find all kinds of ways to make you believe that you can't part with them. You don't need their money, support, talents, connections, pseudopartnering, or "coparenting." For them, it's about winning; it's not about caring. The longer you stay, the more it will cost you in the end.

6. The best way to deal with a sociopath is . . . *not to!* No matter what anyone tells you, you don't need to take care of a sociopath's feelings. Such people don't *have* real feelings to hurt, but *you* do. And you can get destroyed by trying too hard to stay involved or be nice.

7. Don't try to fix what never worked. Don't allow yourself to keep giving chances to someone with no conscience. He will never change! He'll take advantage of your generosity and forgiving nature. Choose to help only people who want to change . . . yourself included.

8. Never cover for the sociopath again. Don't allow yourself to hide the sociopath's true nature from anyone. Your job is to take care of *you*. You don't owe him anything. *He* is responsible for the consequences of *all* his own actions.

9. There is a reason you got here and a gift in your betrayal. If you're involved with a sociopath, you can and will learn why you created this bond. You can and will grow into great joy as you gain knowledge about and move on from this painful chapter of your life. Allow yourself to welcome this explosion of your world. Trust me—getting out of *this* pit is a blessing.

In Closing

Let's review the primary lesson of this chapter. You could be married to, or involved with, a sociopath. Sociopaths destroy people. You can't possibly heal your life if such a person is part of it. If one is, you've probably hidden from yourself the full truth of your partner's danger to you. You've hoped, prayed, and replayed ancient trauma bonds destined to harm you more and more.

Now it's time to come clean. Ask yourself if you're involved with sociopath. Figure out the answer once and for all. And if it's *yes,* do whatever it takes to get out. I guarantee you—you won't be sorry. In fact, you'll eventually be glad. You'll get to the point where you won't even be able to comprehend how you could have possibly stayed in that awful place for so long. Your life will be so much better. You'll be free! . . . And in the next chapter, you'll explore how you got to where you are, and what you're meant to learn from it.

Chapter 4

HOW DID YOU GET HERE, AND WHAT ARE YOU MEANT TO LEARN FROM THIS?

$\mathcal{W}$hether you realize it or not, you created the life you're living. Your unique inborn nature and the lessons you learned growing up prepared you to do just what you've done up until now. And, as I'm sure you know, some of what you've brought upon yourself doesn't serve you very well at all. Of course, you have the power to change all of it going forward, but you need to understand how you got here in the first place if you're going to be successful in doing that.

What's Your Story?

So, how did you get here, and what are you meant to learn from this? This is the "Monday-morning quarterback" chapter, the *Hindsight is twenty-twenty* teaching, the postmortem examination. This is your opportunity to look back on the history of your relationship from a new perspective. Today you have information you didn't have before. You know where your story, which started sometime in the past, has taken you. And you know a lot of things about yourself, and your partner, that you didn't recognize, realize, register, or have the wisdom to trust.

You got to this point for some reason. You're a product of your genetics, feelings, impulses, hormones, neurobiology, unique gifts and vulnerabilities, personality traits, beliefs, and ideas, as well as the lessons of your upbringing. You'll learn more about some of those determinants later in this chapter. But for now, I want you to start looking back and considering the following questions. I've created a list for self-reflection that taps into many common themes:

Questions for Self-Reflection

- Were you too anxious to find a partner?
- Did you agree to the first proposal that came your way even if it wasn't the best fit?
- Did you "settle" for your mate?
- Have you been too quick to believe in him or trust him?
- Did you give your partner the benefit of the doubt when, perhaps, you shouldn't have done so?
- Did you get married to please your parents?
- Did you commit when you were too young to understand what you were doing, and stay in the relationship because it took a long time to figure out what being married really meant?
- Did you make decisions to commit to or stay in your relationship from a place of fear . . . fear about abandonment, a ticking biological clock, finances, or child support and care?
- Did you commit because that step in your life was "supposed" to come next: go to school . . . get job . . . get married?

- Did you get married because you had already sent out invitations and made wedding plans? Or did you stay because your parents gave you big fancy wedding?

- Did you tolerate unhappiness in your partnership for years without realizing its significance?

- Did you isolate yourself from friends and relatives who might have offered you a useful perspective or some support?

- Were you *too* giving or thoughtful?

- Did you keep secrets?

- Did you forgive the unforgivable?

- Did you stay with a philanderer for a long time, hoping he would change?

- Did you try too hard? Or not hard enough?

- Did you expect too much, or too little, back?

- Were you too responsible . . . or not responsible enough?

- Did you push your sexual needs down, disconnect from them, or experience unmet desires?

- Did you view sexual activity as a duty as opposed to a pleasure?

- Were you sexual when you didn't want to be . . . or in ways that were uncomfortable for you?

- Did you stay in the relationship for sex, even if the rest of your partnership was bad?

- Did you keep setting deadlines for changes that needed to occur, yet stay even though nothing got better?

- Were you used or abused?

- Did you stay because of what other people might say if you left?

- Were you taught to see longevity of marriage as a virtue . . . no matter what?

- Did you look to your partner to complete you? To make you happy? To meet *all* of your needs?

- Did you choose, or stay with, a gorgeous guy *because* he was gorgeous—even though he treated you badly?

- Were you trying to be everything to your partner?

- Were you living someone else's model?

- Did you find yourself using food, alcohol, spending/shopping, or any other behavior to self-soothe because you were *so* unhappy or *so* anxious?

- Were you honest and open with your partner? Was he with you?

- Did you doubt yourself too much or not enough?

- Did being in the relationship become habitual or routine? Did you stay in it without thinking?

- Were you too self-critical, or too critical of your partner?

- Are there things you wish you'd known sooner?

- Were you too polite and ladylike—that is, careful not to offend?

- Were you the person you wanted to be?

- Just who *do* you want to be?

- What do you hope to change going forward?

I'd like you to keep your responses to the preceding questions in mind as you move on to learn about the origin of self-concept and the role of intuition in development. It's important that you understand how you got to this point so that you can accept and forgive yourself, act differently, and create your heart's desire. Let's start by looking at the role of upbringing in shaping your current-day experiences.

The Origins of Self-Concept

The lessons we learn about ourselves in childhood determine our self-concepts as adults. The models we're exposed to or taught during our formative years dramatically affect our mind-sets. For most of us, our primary places of learning are our families of origin. We discover how to think about ourselves and others from what our parents teach us by word and example. And, as you know from the prior chapter, our life experiences actually influence the development of our brain structures.

As children, we learn and store away information with the degree of cognitive understanding we have at the time of the lesson. So, for example, if we're young and still very concrete or literal in our thinking, we may simply absorb a lesson like: *I am a bad boy* or *I am a naughty girl.* Since our capacity to understand what might make a person good or bad hasn't yet been developed, we file away the information as a simple fact.

Without being consciously aware of these stored self-concepts, we're influenced by them throughout our adult lives. Since these old ways of thinking can cause dysfunction and intense pain, we may find ourselves questioning our ideas and choices enough to identify some of our negative core beliefs over time. Having identified them, we can use our adult modes of perception to talk back to our childlike ones. By recognizing and subsequently challenging our internalized beliefs, we can change and replace them with more constructive and positive ideas. This healing process involves using a cognitive-behavioral technique—a form of self-talk called *affirmations*—to reprogram destructive mind-sets. You'll find out more about that technique in Chapter 7.

But before you learn how to change your mind-set, you need to discover how those negative lessons actually affect you. What do you do with them? What does it really mean to be influenced by your past?

Strange as the idea may seem, we all reexperience our pasts in the present. Having been called stupid or lazy in childhood, we may tell ourselves we're *stupid* or *lazy* now. We may find our self-concepts and worldviews reflected back in the words of others, even when those people aren't saying what we think we hear. So we can *hear* our friends or bosses calling us dumb or unmotivated, when they're simply following up with us to determine where we are with a project.

Additionally, we re-create familiar family dynamics in our adult relationships, even if those dynamics were, and still are, painful to us. We may pick critical friends, bosses, lovers, and life partners. We may set up situations where we're trying to fix the unfixable. What is familiar somehow feels right! Our brains get programmed to relive what was already experienced. Hence the popular notion that "many women marry their fathers" and "men marry their mothers."

In spite of our adult desires to experience joy, fulfillment, and pleasure in our relationships and pursuits, we often unknowingly re-create the pain, sadness, and loss from our childhoods. We do it minute to minute by what we tell ourselves, and year by year as a result of the life choices we make. Our biggest personal challenge can be trying to figure out how to live the life we're meant to live, as opposed to the one someone else might have taught us to re-create.

You've probably heard the expression *You are your own worst enemy.* I believe this statement to be true. We are, in many ways, what we believe. Both my personal life and clinical work with patients have shown me how frequently our troubles result from self-sabotage. We often impose limits on ourselves that trap us into living what doesn't work. Until, and unless, we identify and challenge our beliefs and patterns, we remain stuck in unproductive, even self-destructive, positions.

Some of your counterproductive thoughts are easy to identify; while others are deeply buried, hidden from your conscious knowledge. The ideas that are readily accessible are the ones you hear in your head. For instance, your internal voice might say, *That was a stupid thing to do,* or *You are such a loser.* You can discover these accessible beliefs by attending to the dialogue in your mind. But identifying your deeply buried beliefs requires more digging. It involves examining your destructive life patterns and tracking their origin. What did you learn that you're unconsciously playing out? You need to do some detective work to discover the underlying beliefs that you haven't given voice to yet. The questions at the beginning and end of this chapter are designed to help you do just that.

The Role of Intuition

One of the most important lessons I took out of my training to become a psychiatrist is this: *the most crucial things I need to know about a patient show themselves to me in our very first meeting.* Since all of us are consistent, my patients would arrive with their issues, "stuff," and stories every day. And if I were a good enough detective/listener, I could figure out from the outset a lot about how to understand them in their quests to heal their lives. During my training, I realized that my job was to become adept at learning how to see, hear, feel, and understand the significance of what my patients were showing me. Everything that mattered would be there from the beginning. (Of course, I learned this lesson after medical school and many years after I got married.)

This lesson is true for all of us, every day of our lives. We each bring our whole self into every interaction. We're registering, putting out, and processing all kinds of information from the first second we see, hear, and meet one another.

So, for example, from the moment you became involved with your partner, you were gleaning and sending out many signals. And, chances are, if you're in a relationship that has exploded on you, then you pushed down, minimized, or ignored some of the warning signs that were there from the beginning.

Our intuition is brilliant, and oftentimes we make bad decisions because we don't pay enough attention to it. We may deny, downplay, or otherwise silence our wisest selves. And we often do that because of what we've been taught to do. We follow rules that made sense in our childhoods even if they don't serve us very well anymore. We replay ingrained dynamics that we don't even recognize are operative, and we misinterpret our bodies' messages and lessons. We lack the capacity to identify our feelings and/or the ability to know what they're trying to tell us. We do the best we know how to do . . . but our best isn't necessarily the best that *can* be done.

I'll use my own story to illustrate this lesson. I'm sure you'll recall that after I got engaged, I became really depressed.

Although I sought help at the time, I received the wrong guidance. I now know that my body was trying to tell me to get out. I didn't know how to understand what it was telling me then. But that episode occurred eight months into my relationship. What I haven't yet told you was what I initially experienced upon meeting my ex-husband. What actually happened when I saw Peter for the very first time?

I met my ex-husband in January of my first year of medical school, outside one of the lecture-hall buildings of our university. Peter was walking home with a fellow classmate named Matt, a guy I knew whom I was really attracted to. Matt and Peter were in the same class a year ahead of me, and our two classes were to have a party together that evening. Matt introduced me to his companion, and soon thereafter, he excused himself to head off to pick up the beer kegs for that evening's party.

I was left alone with Peter, and I felt really uncomfortable. He looked unkempt, sort of like a caveman, to me. Something about him gave me the heebie-jeebies. We were making our way home in the same direction, so we walked side by side for a few blocks. When he asked me what I liked to do and I told him that I was a runner, he said, "We'll have to go running together sometime." His words really unsettled me for some reason, and I ducked into the next store we passed, saying I needed to buy something there and would see him later. I was relieved to be free . . . but somehow managed to push down the wisdom of my intuition by that evening.

Peter waited to walk me home from the party that night. And I got quickly hooked in as he began sharing his family-of-origin issues . . . his struggles, pain, and challenges. Without realizing what was happening, I stepped full force into the pattern that I'd lived for many years with my mom. I became the confidante, caretaker, problem solver, and trusted friend, in exchange for attention, distraction, companion-ship, and emotional investment.

As you already know, for many years I stayed in what I *now* know was a very dysfunctional and self-destructive relation-ship. At the age of 22, during my traumatic first year of medical school, I stepped into a quicksand-like dynamic that took me a long time to break out of. Old patterns, beliefs, self-doubt, and fears kept me trying to make the unworkable work. And I suffered a great deal in the process. I had no idea what was going on or what to do about it. Over the years, I sought a lot of therapy, but none of it was very good. My patients were the ones who taught me what I really needed to learn.

Today I know about mind-body interactions. I know how to identify feelings and how to figure out what they mean. I'm aware of how important it is to trust our intuitive wisdom and to step fully into the power of possibility rather than allow-ing fear to take charge. I know that our inner healer doesn't lie, and the feelings of discomfort that present themselves to us when we first meet new folks are deep messages from our highest selves. They're meant to protect, save, and heal us. And to ignore them is to put ourselves at grave risk.

Today, I teach these lessons to my children and patients. I write about them in books and talk about them at confer-ences and workshops and on radio and TV. I remind myself every day to look inward and trust my gut.

Had I known to trust my intuitive wisdom when I was 22 years old, I would never have dated or married Peter. My body kept trying to tell me to get out. *The lesson was there from day one. It always is!* I just didn't know how to recognize it. I didn't know what to do with what I was feeling back then. I didn't understand the lesson of this chapter.

Let's review it: You got to where you are for a reason. You're meant to learn from this experience. You can take charge. You can heal and create your heart's desire. You got here by re-creating your history—by ignoring, denying, minimizing, and missing out on some teachings that you now need to claim. Your job is to identify the silent dysfunctional dynamics that continue to affect you. You did your best . . . but it isn't the best you can do. My patients and I have learned to do better over time, and so can you.

I'd like to share another story to illustrate this concept to you. Let's step into Melissa's world together.

The Power of Ancient Beliefs

Melissa's story is about the power of ancient beliefs to derail our lives. It's also about the empowerment possibility available to all of us to reprogram hidden beliefs so that we can live our hearts' desires.

If you've read my second book, *10 Steps to Take Charge of Your Emotional Life*, you already know part of Melissa's story. She came to me to heal her romantic life years after her first marriage ended in divorce. Her ex-husband had had an affair and chosen to repartner with his lover, and she hadn't yet healed.

When Melissa originally came to see me, she was devastated. "Perhaps I haven't fully recovered," she said, "because I shy away from romantic relationships. And whenever I do get involved with someone, I hold myself way back. Eventually he always leaves. It becomes a replay of my marriage experience."

The two of us began sorting out the lessons of her history. What did she believe? Why was she replaying an abandonment dynamic over and over again? Melissa came from a family with a disabled sibling.

She was a good student and a quiet child. Her parents didn't recognize the attention she needed in order to thrive. She was often expected to take care of her brother, having to put aside her schoolwork and whatever else she wanted to do. As a result, Melissa learned the lesson *My needs aren't important; I have to help those less fortunate, no matter what the cost to me.*

When it came to relationship issues in her adult life, that internalized idea exerted its silent power. During Melissa's courtship, she often played the passive caretaker, putting up with and even accommodating her partner's troubling behavior. When he proposed, her inner-wisdom voice said, *Don't do it!* But her dysfunctional belief countered with *You can't hurt his feelings. He's a nice enough guy. He needs you. You have to say yes.* Without recognizing that the childhood message *My needs are not important; I have to help those less fortunate* was at play, she said yes.

Upon entering the marriage, she buried the message of her inner wisdom, along with her turmoil and misgivings. She tried to make things work, but out of sight and mind is *not* out of life. In spite of her efforts to build a loving partnership, she couldn't alter what she'd known to be true: her husband wasn't ready for, and wouldn't fully commit to, the union.

When he left, Melissa was devastated. She didn't remember that she'd had her own misgivings from the very beginning. She personalized his decision. She told herself she wasn't good enough for him and then carried this sense of low self-worth into subsequent relationships. She dated unavailable men who'd never get close enough to hurt her so deeply again.

It took Melissa and me months to identify the crippling belief that had been behind her acceptance of the marriage proposal. But by looking at her childhood, we finally figured out where the idea had come from. Armed with this knowledge, we began to reprogram the self-destructive brain circuit.

As an adult, Melissa understood the importance of caring for herself and her own needs in life. She came to recognize that she'd abandoned herself in choosing to enter a marriage that wasn't meant to be. The demise of the union was inevitable. *She* was good enough, but she'd made the wrong choice. *It* wasn't right! She'd set herself up to suffer when she ignored her inner wisdom and enacted the learned belief. She had put her own needs aside to avoid "hurting" his feelings. As a result, she had unknowingly hurt herself.

Her internal script needed to be rewritten. It became: *My inner wisdom is my guide. I must honor my feelings, give them voice, and act on them. I am meant to silence the voices that tell me I do not count. Those are not really mine. I am good enough, and deserve to experience joy.*

Melissa and I worked together for some time. She needed to develop skill in identifying and heeding the wisdom of her inner voice, ferreting out and challenging the old belief and living more authentically. Throughout her work, she repeated the new script she'd created. This exercise enabled her to reprogram the old tape, as she strove to believe what she now knew to be true. She graduated from my care several years ago, feeling empowered and transformed.

The universe acts in synergistic and strange ways sometimes. When I was writing Melissa's story for my second
book, I hadn't heard from her in a while. Perhaps we'd connected two or three times since her "graduation." Yet, as I
was writing *about* her, she was writing *to* me. Within days
of putting my old patient's story on paper, I received a New
Year's greeting card from her. She had just read my first book
and loved it. She was writing to tell me that, and to let me
know how well she was doing. She reported that she was now
engaged to a wonderful man and was soon to be married! She
had reprogrammed her mind and changed her life. She was
grateful and thrilled to have me share her story in *10 Steps to
Take Charge of Your Emotional Life*.

Now, as I'm writing my third book, I'm delighted to
be able to tell you that Melissa is living her heart's desire.
She's married to the man of her dreams. He has adopted the
daughter whom *she* had adopted as a single mom. She now
has a beloved husband along with a fabulous child. She has
the family she always longed for. She is deliriously happy and
truly grateful. If *she* can get there, so can you.

Take-Home Points

There's a reason why you got to where you are right now.
It has to do with your nature, beliefs, patterns, and choices.
While you've done your best to care for yourself until now,
some of what you've chosen, and some of what you've been
living, hasn't served you very well.

If you've chosen and stayed with a partner who is actually
a wrong fit for you today, you need to identify the beliefs and
patterns that previously led you to do so. If you've chosen and
stayed with someone who may still be right for you, you need

to figure out how the two of you got to this moment of crisis in your relationship and what each of you is going to think, say, and do differently so that your life together will be better going forward. You must work to accept your history and fallibility. I guarantee you that when your life explodes in betrayal, you are not the victim. Yes, you've been victimized, but somehow you participated in getting to this moment. Learn, accept, and forgive yourself for your role. Your healing depends on your claiming your part and your power.

I suggest that you take some time to think about the lessons of your upbringing and history. Review the questions at the beginning of this chapter. Ponder these ones as well:

- *What am I afraid of?*

- *How do I see myself?*

- *Do I feel bad or guilty sometimes?
  When and why?*

- *Whose voice do I hear in my head?
  Does it serve me well?*

- *Am I hopeful or pessimistic? Do I expect the
  best or worst from others?*

- *How do I view my needs? Feelings? History? Beliefs?*

- *Do I like myself enough? Do I know who I
  am and how I feel most of the time?*

- *Do I honor my intuitive wisdom?*

- *How much do I allow old tapes to run my life?*

- *What ideas, patterns, and beliefs did I learn in childhood? Which ones serve me well, and
  which ones harm me?*

- *What did I learn to ignore or downplay?*

- *What did I learn that I cherish?*

- *What do I value?*

- *Does my life reflect what matters to me?*

- *What role did I play in the explosion of my life?*

I've created a product (available through **www.Hay House.com** or **www.Amazon.com**) called *What Am I Feeling, and What Does It Mean?: A Kit for Self-Growth and Healthy Relationships.* You might want to get yourself a copy. It contains a guidebook, journal, over 250 refrigerator magnets, 22 beautiful cards, and a CD . . . all designed to teach you how to identify and honor your feelings for self-growth. It can help you create and nurture the relationships and the love you most want in life. It's chock-full of communication techniques. And most important of all, it will teach you how to make the connection between your feelings and your intuitive wisdom.

Using the kit may help you own the lesson of this chapter and make it more real. It's really a crucial one. Your life exploded for some reason . . . and by discovering who you are and what your role was in your history, you can change your life for the better! I urge you to use whatever tools you need to help you grow. You might, for instance, want to pursue some counseling or therapy to master this "history" lesson. Many have found that kind of assistance invaluable.

You deserve a life of joy! In the next chapter, we'll look at the role of forgiveness in healing your life when your world explodes.

❋❋❋ ❋❋❋

Chapter 5

WHAT IS THE ROLE OF
FORGIVENESS IN HEALING?

*M*ost books about betrayal focus on forgiveness, on forgiving the offender and yourself. But that concerns me. As I mentioned in the Introduction, I think that the attention on forgiveness is misguided. Trying to forgive can distract you from the work you need to do. Additionally, it's often a fruitless endeavor.

The healing of a wound is a slow and demanding process. It consumes a lot of energy. It won't be until you're far along the way in transcending your pain that you may be able to *begin* forgiving your perpetrator. You can't do so sooner.

What Does Our Culture Tell Us about Forgiveness?

What I've just said may seem blasphemous. It flies in the face of our long-standing beliefs and cultural attitudes. Forgiveness is important. We hear about it all the time. Every religion extols its virtues. Many popular books and gurus emphasize its value. One of the first phrases many of us learn as children, soon after the "please" and "thank you" lesson, is "I'm sorry." Parents and teachers spend a lot of time drilling the significance of being polite, apologizing, and forgiving into our little heads. And, of course, "I'm sorry" and "I forgive you" are what we're supposed to say to one another right away. The offending action and the resolution interaction are meant to occur during a 5- to 15-minute school-recess period or over the speedy dinner "hour."

Learning the difference between right and wrong, as well as the importance of *empathy,* or putting ourselves into others' shoes to see how they might feel when they've been hurt or wronged, is crucial. We need to be taught how to be caring, respectful, and responsible citizens. Our survival as a species depends on the viability of loving, interdependent relationships and communities. We need one another. Life is surely not about any one of us in particular.

Generosity is a virtue. Nursing our own wounds "too much" is considered selfish. We hear "Get over it" or "What's the big deal?" often in our culture. We're not meant to lavish too much attention or energy on our own selves. In fact, we're considered "babies" if we appear to be doing so.

We are to be Christlike or Dalai Lama–like. As Jesus was being crucified, he prayed for those who wronged him: "Father, forgive them; for they know not what they do." The Dalai Lama suggested to Americans outraged by China's seizure of Tibet, "We must pray for the Chinese." We're all taught to love our neighbors as ourselves. We're encouraged to forgive and forget. In doing so, we are taught, we receive healing.

Well, the truth of the matter is we *are* healed when we forgive. In fact, we're transformed, elevated, and deeply calmed when we do so. And forgiving others settles our nervous systems, decreases our blood pressure, and brings upon us a greater sense of peace and joy than being forgiven ourselves does. So, this act is actually good for our health and healing.

But as we all know from wise King Solomon, there is a time and place for everything. There is a time to reap and a time to sow, a time for joy and a time to weep . . . and so on. And there is a time and a place for forgiveness in the betrayal experience, but it's surely not in the beginning, or often anywhere *near* it.

What Is Forgiveness, Anyway?

All of this talk about forgiveness invites the question: *What is forgiveness, anyway?* What does it really mean to forgive someone? In *Spiritual Evolution,* by George E. Vaillant, M.D., there is a great discussion of forgiveness. I've paraphrased the definition in italics: *A willingness to let go of resentment, judgment, or uncaring behavior toward someone who has wrongfully harmed us . . . while nurturing the unearned qualities of love, caring, and giving toward that person.*

In order to forgive, we have to be able to give up our own self-righteousness, moral indignation, anger, rage, and desire for revenge. We have to be able to empathize with the one who has wronged us and be able to see a hopeful future for ourselves. This can be quite a challenge when we've been betrayed.

Forgiveness is an emotional experience. It can't be legislated, commanded, or forced. We're not in conscious control of forgiving. It's true that our capacity to forgive increases with maturity. The older we are, the easier it can be for us to do so. In our youth we're driven by our own identity development and by competition. We discover who we are in this way. But our focus shifts over time: As we become less passionate about *winning* and *being right,* it becomes easier to forgive one another. We realize we're all human.

Beware of Forgiving Too Fast

While maturity may increase the capacity to forgive, there are other elements involved in determining it. Pay attention to this lesson because what I'm about to tell you is really crucial to your health. *You can't, and shouldn't, try to get to forgiveness too soon.* Sometimes your survival depends on holding on to your anger, sense of moral indignation, and pain. Many of us have silenced our intuition; replayed bad dynamics with problematic partners; and stayed in relationships with hurtful, and even dangerous, men because we were too caring, self-sacrificing, or quick to forgive.

Beware of forgiving too fast . . . or of thinking you *ought* to forgive. Healing your life after betrayal means suspending your desire to make it right between you and your partner. Let go of your belief that you ought to forgive and forget. And don't let anyone convince you that this is necessary to healing your life. It's not! Taking charge *is.* Using your anger for personal empowerment *is.* Fueling your growth trajectory is what's most important. It's about you . . . not him.

There is a difference between banishing blame and forgiving someone. To heal your life, you do need to banish blame. Remember that you're not a victim. You do have to figure out what your role has been in your history and attend to growing yourself in order to move forward. But you don't need to let go of all resentment, judgment, or indifference in order to heal. It might even be necessary for you to keep them active for a while. And you surely don't have to foster caring and loving feelings toward your partner. You may never be able to do that, and it's okay if you can't.

True forgiveness can only occur *after* you've begun to heal. You can't rush it. The process is helped if forgiveness is a two-way street. In other words, it will be easier for you to forgive someone who apologizes and is remorseful, but a sorry perpetrator doesn't automatically lead to forgiveness in the one who has been harmed. And you don't need him to be sorry to be able to forgive him.

What Forgiveness Is Not

Now I want to tell you what forgiveness is *not*. According to George Vaillant, forgiveness is *not* accepting the unacceptable. You may be angry for years but not vengeful.

Forgiveness is *not* forgetting. You may never forget what was done to you. In fact, holding on to memories of dangers you've lived is self-protective. Remembering keeps you from repeating self-destructive dynamics.

Forgiveness is *not* giving up your right to justice. In fact, you may need to seek restitution of some kind for the wrongs that have been done to you. You may even need to resort to legal recourse to get support or help in your healing.

Forgiveness does *not* remove or alter pain from the past. The hurt and sorrow of yesterday can't be changed. Forgiveness can only make your present and future less painful.

And, perhaps most crucial of all, *forgiveness in no way excuses the wrongdoer.* When you're ready to forgive, you do so for yourself. His inexcusable behavior stays inexcusable. Forgiveness isn't about him. As I've mentioned, it's only about, and for, *you.*

My Story of Forgiveness

Let me make these concepts real with an example. I'll use my own story to make the points. You already know that I lived through a very disturbing relationship dynamic with my mother. And, of course, her behavior affected my development of identity and my choice of a life partner. I stayed in a miserable marriage for years largely because of what I learned to do from my mom. And up until the day she died seven years ago, I can't recall her ever admitting she was wrong or sorry about anything.

While I do hold my mother responsible for what she did and taught, I never blamed her for my challenges. I was often hurt by, and angry with, her, but I took on the responsibility of creating my own life . . . imperfect as it was. And for a very long time, I didn't know about the lesson of Chapter 4. I didn't know about the power of upbringing to affect brain development and life choices. I didn't have an awareness of how much damage she had inadvertently done.

As my marriage deteriorated and I learned more and more about what I was replaying, I began to appreciate the toxicity of some of what I'd lived in my earlier years. It made me angry, but it wasn't until my mom was long gone that my life exploded in betrayal. And when my world shattered, I hadn't yet forgiven her. Interestingly enough, it was my betrayal experience with Peter, and all the issues I had worked through with my father by that time, that ultimately enabled me to forgive my mother!

What do I mean by this? And how could betrayal by a man who was somewhat like my mother have enabled me to forgive *her?* Well, first of all, my dad and I had already processed a lot of my upbringing history. In my father's final years, he'd realized, and had taken ownership for, his role in abandoning me to my mother's sickness. So, we had visited a lot of past pain together, grieved for it, and forgiven one another for all that had transpired. I'd been healed by that process.

Then when my life exploded in betrayal, I was able to see quite clearly how alike, *and how different,* Peter and my mom were. While I'd replayed a familiar childhood dynamic with my ex-husband, my mother had truly loved me and would never have put me at risk in the way Peter had. In fact, it was largely because of the financial resources my parents had given and left me that I was able to get out of my marriage! So forgiveness of my mom, seven years after her death, became one of the gifts of my betrayal . . . and it happened all by itself. It couldn't be forced. And until the death of my marriage, I hadn't even known if it would *ever* occur.

Timing Is Everything

Lots of books about betrayal focus on the importance of forgiveness in healing. And it's possible that you'll eventually forgive the person who has wronged you. The gift of forgiveness will come when, and only when, the time is right for you. It's likely you'll have done lots of personal processing and growth work by the time you're ready. I've seen that reality play out hundreds of times in my clinical practice.

Mary, one of my long-term patients, forgave her ex-husband 18 years after being betrayed by him. And her transformation came upon her by surprise. Her daughter had just graduated from high school. Mary had started a graduate-school program and begun to see a new future for herself. And then, "out of the blue," the miracle occurred! Her experience isn't unusual. You may have one like it.

Only when you've moved way beyond the intensity of your trauma and gained a new perspective can the miracle of forgiveness occur. I'll refer to *Eat, Pray, Love* again. Elizabeth Gilbert goes all the way to an ashram in India to learn the lesson of personal transformation. She describes the beautiful spiritual ritual she's given that ultimately allows her to forgive and be forgiven. It's only effective *after* she's gotten out of the marriage; given her ex-husband all of her possessions; let go of the illusion of control; and asked, begged, and prayed for an inner shift. She releases anger, resentment, and blame. Forgiveness comes to her when she's ready to receive it. She forgives her ex-husband and herself.

What Does It Mean to Forgive Yourself?

You're probably wondering: *What does it mean to forgive myself? And how does <u>self</u>-forgiveness relate to what's usually meant by "forgiveness" or to what I've read so far in this chapter?*

Well, forgiving yourself is a different process/phenomenon. When we therapists talk about forgiving yourself, we're encouraging you to be gentle, loving, accepting, and nonjudgmental of yourself. We're reminding you that you've done your best job until now. You didn't know any better. There is a reason for your actions and shortcomings. You can learn and change. And your transformation can only occur from a place of compassion for yourself.

We're probably using the wrong term because we don't view you as someone who has "wronged" yourself. We see you as a wonderful, imperfect being who can be too self-critical or hard on herself sometimes. And we're encouraging you to be lighter on, and more loving of, yourself. So we say "Forgive yourself" . . . but perhaps we shouldn't, because those words can be really confusing to you—and to all of us, it seems—in the work of moving beyond betrayal.

So, what is the place of forgiving yourself in healing your life when your world explodes? Well, if "forgiving" language works for you, use it. Each time you visit a flaw, error, or limitation in yourself, say, "I forgive you for your mistake," or something similar. And let it really be okay!

But if forgiving language doesn't cut it for you, *don't use it*. It isn't necessary for you to do so. Perhaps you'd like to remind yourself that you did the best you could have done. You might prefer to focus on honoring, loving, or cherishing yourself on your way to wholeness. If those concepts are hard for you, try visualizing someone who loves you comforting you when you feel self-critical and scared. Or read affirming books and cards; listen to CDs that reassure you; or call a friend, lover, confidante, or therapist. Choose to "forgive" yourself in your own language and in your own way.

Please be gentle with yourself as you review your history and your mistakes. As you learn your lessons, keep in mind that you're going through hell. You're not alone. Many of us have been there. And we know how hard it can be to get through this nightmare without adding insult to injury . . . or becoming our own worst enemies. There is light at the end of your tunnel. Keep fueling yourself with compassion and love. You *will* get there. And you'll stand in brightness, in your full radiance.

Don't let yourself get derailed by believing you need to forgive him too soon . . . or at all! You don't! In fact, many of my patients, friends, and colleagues have needed regular validation of the egregious nature of their betrayal experiences in order to keep themselves out of harm's way. I've supported lots of women as they fought against their instincts to be guilted into reentering the lion's den. I've reminded them of their own histories to keep them from repeating their past trauma experiences.

I've been the voice of reason; I've challenged abused women when they've said, "I have to give him another chance." I've questioned them about what it means to be loyal when they've had sex against their will and told me: "I can't say no—he's my husband!" I've had to remind some patients of how often they've been misused or mistreated by their partners or how miserable they've been in their relationship dynamics. I've done this to care for them.

Because many of us are too quick to doubt and criticize ourselves and tell ourselves we're making mountains out of molehills, we believe that we need to forgive and forget or tell ourselves that what's awful is no big deal! Healing requires us to be open to self-love and the voice of reason. And we need others to give us perspective.

I urge you to surround yourself with people who will support you in that way. It's part of loving or "forgiving" yourself on your way to wholeness, and you deserve joy. It's your gift and birthright! You *can* live your heart's desire. And, in the next chapter, you'll begin learning to trust in your ability to create the life you really want!

Chapter 6

TRUST IN YOUR ABILITY TO
CREATE YOUR HEART'S DESIRE

*A*s the title would imply, this chapter is designed to teach how to trust in your ability to create your heart's desire. And it's a really crucial lesson because if you're reading this book, it's likely you've been burned, jolted, destabilized, and challenged by betrayal. You've lived a lot of hell and want to experience great joy. You're probably afraid of loneliness, isolation, or an inability to take care of yourself and those you love. You may be fearful of the future, of the present, or of reliving your past!

You're worried. And all of your concerns are to be expected. "Normal" people have them. I did. My patients do. Why not you, too? Having been around this bend many times, I want to reassure you. I believe in you. I trust in your ability to create a fabulous future for yourself.

The Power of Possibility

You can live your dream. But there's a catch: You'll only be able to get there if you actually believe it's possible. Whatever you believe will happen is *going* to happen! Your life is a self-fulfilling prophecy. Your thoughts create your experiences.

What you attend to, think about, and focus on, you bring about—whether or not it's your conscious desire to do so!

What do I mean by that statement? Well, if you've read my second book, *10 Steps to Take Charge of Your Emotional Life*, you'll remember the ninth step: *Live in the power of the possible*. Possibility is what I'm talking about here. I use the story *The Little Engine That Could* to demonstrate the importance of *trusting* in miracles if you're to bring them about in your life. Living your dreams requires you to challenge your negativity, false assumptions, and laziness. It means letting go of ideas that hold you hostage, such as *I can't, They won't, It's hopeless,* or *It will never work*. It involves shutting down the *It's too much effort—it's not worth it* or *Why bother?* inner dialogue. It demands that you step fully into your hopes, prayers, and dreams.

You know those famous sayings: *We are such stuff as dreams are made on; If you build it, they will come; I have a dream;* and *The only thing we have to fear is fear itself.* You have a sense of the power of hope and faith to transform lives. And you probably know that your future depends on your belief in your tomorrows.

Perhaps you hope for inner peace, more free time, a life partner, children, career success, self-acceptance, self-love, good health, financial security, joy, a pet, a garden, or a dwelling that really feels like home. Whatever it is, it's possible . . . but you may not believe that. You might even be too afraid to allow yourself to contemplate the possibility. You most likely apply "impossible" assessments to yourself such as: *Get real, Who are you kidding,* and *That will never happen.* You probably cut yourself off from realizing your dreams before you even get started naming them. We all do that sometimes.

Devote some thought to how you shut down your wishes for your life. How do you extinguish hope? What do you say?

Well, of course, living your dreams requires you to banish your naysayers, hope killers, and doom-and-gloom voices. It demands that you stop saying things like *I can't find a life partner* if you desire one. You must replace negative ideas with faith that you'll find your heart's desire. So, how are you to do that? Well, you need to learn what negative brain circuits are and how to reprogram them. Let's step into that lesson now.

Reprogramming Negative Brain Circuits

Perhaps you have some experience with affirmations or other cognitive-behavioral techniques. These methods are extremely powerful in altering problematic brain circuits because they work by creating new neural pathways. You see, when you tell yourself something over and over, the same pattern of neurons fires repeatedly. Eventually, that circuit takes on a life of its own. So when you encounter the familiar situation, your brain begins to tell you what it already knows (almost without thinking). After feeding yourself something negative for years, such as *My needs aren't important,* your mind has that thought pretty well fixed in place.

But you can change this! The way to do so is by telling yourself something different over and over again until *it* becomes ingrained. You don't have to think the new message is true for it to take; you just have to keep saying it. After a while, it will become fixed enough that you'll believe it instead.

There's something else I need to teach you about the strength of your thoughts to affect your life. It concerns the minute-to-minute power of your mind-body connection.

Whenever you give yourself encouraging or positive messages, internal chemicals are released that calm the deep limbic system of your brain. This makes you feel happy and relaxed.

By contrast, when you focus on sad, angry, worrisome, or critical thoughts, your brain releases chemicals that activate your limbic system and make you feel tense, anxious, and unsettled. So even before you reprogram your problematic circuits, you can harm or heal yourself by what you allow your mind to "say."

In this chapter, you'll be learning how to banish negativity and foster belief in your dreams. The first step of that process is for you to make a list of your imprisoning beliefs or negative thoughts. Please take some time to do that. Your list might include statements like "I'm too fat," "I'm not enough," or "I can't succeed." Make the list as long as you wish, and feel free to add to it as you notice other ideas you think of.

Once you have your negative-thoughts list, it's time to start developing positive, affirming thoughts to speak back to your internal critic. This exercise involves taking each negative idea on your list and fashioning an uplifting antidote in response.

How do you decide what sort of statements to create? Well, here are some guidelines to follow:

1. All affirmations need to be in the present tense. So let's suppose that the negative statement on your list is "I'm a failure." Rather than saying *I will be successful,* you might try: *I am successful* or *My best is good enough.*

2. Write statements that are positive rather than negative. For example, if your imprisoning belief is "No one will ever love me," your antidote might be something such as *I am lovable and loved,* as opposed to *I am not going to be abandoned.*

3. Your validating statement doesn't need to be believable to you at this moment. In fact, it probably won't be or you wouldn't have to create and say it. The affirmation is something you choose to say now in order to bring about changes in your belief system and in what comes to you in the future as a result.

Let's practice this exercise. Take your list of negative thoughts and start writing positive antidotes for each one. Here are some examples:

- "I'm fat and ugly" becomes *My body serves me well* or *I appreciate the miracle of my body.*

- "I can't take care of myself" becomes *There's always help; there's always hope.*

- "People are scary" or "The world is unsafe" becomes *I am at one, at peace, and at ease. The universe provides for me.*

- "I won't be happy until I have financial security" becomes *I am comfortable and safe. Abundance is mine for the asking.*

- "I'm a nobody" becomes *I am a blessed child of the universe.*

- "I'm weak" becomes *I am vibrant, energetic, and empowered.*

- "I'm alone" becomes *I am held in the warm embrace of the infinite.*

- "I should be more outgoing or friendly" becomes *I am wonderful just as I am.*

- "I'm scared" becomes *I am safe in the universe. I do not fear.*

- "My anxiety will escalate out of control" becomes *I have tools to use to interrupt my anxiety.*

- "I am destined to fail" becomes *I create my own destiny, and I live in the moment.*

Sometimes finding the proper affirmation or antidote to a self-imprisoning thought takes a while. Don't get discouraged. Instead, sleep on it, get help, and experiment. The right answer will be revealed.

Once you've created affirmations for each of your negative ideas, write these positive statements on index cards—these will become your reprogramming tool. But how are you to use them? Each morning and evening, take three deep belly breaths, thank the universe for giving you the power to heal, and then read the statements on your cards. Say each one out loud three times before going on to the next, letting the words sink into your being. When you're finished, thank the universe again for supporting you, and then go on with your day.

It's crucial that you read your affirmations regularly. Remember that you're up against entrenched ideas. Each time you affirm these new thoughts, you'll feel the immediate, self-soothing benefits. Over time, you'll alter your mind-set loops and dramatically change your life.

Identifying What You Really Want

Now that you know how to identify and reprogram negative brain circuits, you're well on your way to trusting your ability to create your heart's desire. But you need to do something else to facilitate that process. You have to begin identifying what you actually want. So, start asking yourself what you hope for, dream of, and most ardently desire. You must give your passion your attention.

I guarantee you that you can be successful . . . but you have to work at it. I know that truth from working with patients like Melissa (whose story was discussed in Chapter 4). And I know it from my own experience. I'll use *my* story again to show you what I mean.

I was in an unhappy marriage for many years, and two years before it exploded, I started actively working on creating my heart's desire. I began with Laura Day's book *Practical Intuition*. And I used the tools in it to clarify where I was and what I hoped for. A year later, I began working with the instruction book *Your Heart's Desire,* created by my trusted colleague Sonia Choquette.

In her book, Sonia walks you through nine principles necessary to create the life you want . . . and it won't surprise you to learn that the first one is: *Bring your dream into focus.* In other words, you have to identify and focus on what you desire right now, because you create what you attend to. And in order to create your heart's desire, you have to be very clear about exactly what you want. Sonia instructs her readers to rank their desires in order of priority from a list of ten. One of the items is a special intention that you express in writing, and she also asks you to jot down some sentences about what you desire in each of the ten areas.

I'm going to share some of my responses to her exercises with you because I want you to see how awesome intention is in creating miracles. From reading the Introduction to this book, you know my story. You know where I was and where I am; I was in a miserable marriage, and I'm happier now than I've ever been. And I'm sure my joy will continue to grow. But how did I get here?

Well, for one thing, I followed Sonia's suggestions and made a priority list. My #1, or special intention, was to have a "soul mate/life partner for once," and I placed the importance of relationships as #2 on my list. Under the relationships section, I wrote: "I intend to have a more loving and intimate romance (marriage?) relationship and a growing sphere of close friends with whom I feel fully at ease." Elsewhere in the intention section I wrote: "I intend to separate myself from my ex-husband's toxicity—whatever that means I have to do." Looking back over time, I've come to recognize the fundamental nature of this intention for me. In fact, my "dearest wish" when I worked with Laura Day's book the year before was a "loving partnership."

It's important for you to understand that some of your heart's desires have been with you forever and are consistent over time. Do you know what they are and why you haven't created them yet?

Sonia's second principle is: *Gain the support of your subconscious mind.* This is another dimension of what it means to believe in your dreams. Your conscious desire and your subconscious mind must be in agreement. For instance, if your heart's desire is a loving relationship, your subconscious mind can't be saying: "I don't deserve true love." If a mixed message like that exists, you won't realize your dream. You need alignment. Using affirmations to tackle your subconscious negative beliefs is one way to work this principle. You learned how to do that earlier in this chapter.

Here are some other tools. One of them is what I call *Monitor the company you keep,* and what Sonia calls going "in the direction" of what you want. In other words, surround yourself with people, books, images, and ideas that represent what you desire—that is, joyful relationships, rewarding careers, and so forth. An additional tool is to write a song for

your new beliefs. You must write it—and sing it—to yourself.
Using it is what will make it real!

So, I'm going to show you my song. It helped me combat
fear and trust in my dream. I do feel a little foolish sharing
it . . . but it worked . . . so here goes! (It's sung to the tune of
"I've Gotta Be Me.")

My Song

I've gotta believe
In love being real
In knowing I'll find
My soul mate in time
He'll energize me
And heal my deep wounds
In safety I'll be
With passion and glee
I've gotta be free
I've gotta be me

What song might you write? What fears do you need to
silence? What dreams and ideas do you need to empower?
Perhaps you're wondering if this way of moving in the direction of your truest desires will really work. How long do
you have to do this stuff? And how will the dream actually
materialize?

I want to reassure you: you *will* get there! I've seen the
power of this process over and over again. The more you
step into it, the fuller and faster you'll create what you most
want. But there's no predicting exactly how it will come . . .
or how long it will take. You'll likely be surprised by how well
it works . . . once you're *really* ready!

I'll use my story to demonstrate again. I began creating my heart's desire several years before my marriage exploded. I chose to believe in and nurture the possibility that I would live my dream someday. I used many books, tools, and techniques; and you already know they worked. But how, and how fast?

My current love stepped into my world *four months*—to the day—from the day my life exploded! I wasn't consciously looking for him; in fact, I'd thought it would take me at least a year to meet a man I would deeply love. I absolutely knew it would happen . . . in time. But I never expected the universe to respond as quickly as it did. Unbeknownst to me, one of its spiritual laws had been activated. You see, as I was doing my work, the universe was responding. It will grant us its gifts as soon as we're ready to receive them! I had forgotten, so I was surprised.

I was at my regular gym on a Sunday morning and had just finished my aerobic workout. I went to the paper-towel dispenser to get what I needed to wipe off my machine. I was drenched in sweat and looked like a drowned rat . . . when an amazing thing happened. I got sucked into a powerful energy field! Tom, the man on the elliptical trainer right next to the towel dispenser, struck up a conversation with me. And we were locked in something intense.

When I saw Tom at the gym the next time, he asked me out for coffee . . . which turned into dinner . . . which turned into conversation until 2 A.M.! And to make a long story short, I fell in love with him. I *intended* to find him by believing in my ability to create my heart's desire. At the time, I didn't know if he would be my soul mate—or an angel who had come into my world to teach me the lessons I needed to know to live my greatest desire. But there he was . . . and there I was . . . and we fell deeply in love! You, too, can enter this dream-actualization process and be wildly successful. So, start really asking yourself:

- *What is my dream? My dearest wish?*
  What do I most want and need?

- *What is my song?*

- *What company do I want to keep?*

- *What do I hope and pray for?*

- *What will I tell myself every day from now on?*

- *What is my fabulous future?*

Varied-Volume Affirmation

I suggest you end this lesson with a varied-volume affirmation. It's another useful tool for aligning your dreams and subconscious mind. I'll teach you how to do it.

Here's the affirmation I'd like you to use to practice this technique: *I live my dream.* You'll recite the affirmation out loud five times. The first time, you'll use a loud voice and a lot of emphasis only when you say the first word, *I.* So you'll say: *I live my dream*—where the underlined word is stressed. The second time you say the affirmation, you emphasize the second word, and so on. Your first four affirmations will be like this:

1st time: *I live my dream!*
2nd time: *I LIVE my dream!*
3rd time: *I live MY dream!*
4th time: *I live my DREAM!*

Then you'll say *all four* words in a loud voice and with a lot of emphasis: <u>*I LIVE MY DREAM!*</u>

Do this exercise now. You'll feel an amazing surge of energy and sense of hope when you're through. It's awesome! I often use this tool when working with large audiences to quickly demonstrate their creative power. When hundreds of people do this together, the energy is unbelievable. Everyone feels empowered by it!

You can use any affirmation you want for this exercise, but it works best with short sentences (three or four words) and single-syllable words. Also, it falls flat with an ending such as *it* or *so*.

Pick a varied-volume affirmation statement that speaks to you; use this example or make up your own. Try this technique every day for a few weeks. It will build your faith in your ability to create your heart's desire. In the next chapter, you'll learn how to take further action to create the life you really want.

Chapter 7

TAKE ACTION TO CREATE
THE LIFE YOU REALLY WANT

*A*s the title suggests, this chapter is about taking action to create the life you really want. And the first thing I'm going to tell you to do may sound obvious or ridiculous. "Duh!" you may say when I explain that in order to create the life you really want, you have to do "it" differently. You have to change your ideas, approaches, expectations, and behaviors if you want a different outcome. Here's another spiritual law of the universe: *you'll keep getting what you've gotten if you keep doing what you've done until now!*

Identifying What You Want

So, you have to change. But what does that mean in practice? What do you actually need to change? How do you implement change? And how do you know if you're making the *right* changes for you?

Well, here's where the rubber meets the road, as they say. This is your opportunity to take a deep personal inventory. It's time for you to examine your gifts and limitations, accomplishments and errors, values, wishes, hopes, dreams, aspirations, and aversions. This action lesson involves taking stock of what you truly want to experience and identifying how you've interfered with allowing yourself to be successful in creating your heart's desire.

Let's begin by looking at what it means to be creative. There are some rules you need to know:

1. You'll only be able to manifest the life you want from a place of authenticity. You must engage your intuitive wisdom, wise self, heart's desire, and deepest wishes.

2. No authentic desire can emerge from a place of arrogance, fear, expectation, or judgment or out of a wish to control or to harm. While you can't realize your heart's desire in a destructive, toxic environment, getting yourself out of danger will open the door for your imagination to create what you want.

3. True desires are never about material possessions. They're about meaning and experience.

So, this is the moment to start thinking long and hard about what you want. What do you value? What brings you joy? What do you desire? Begin to imagine it. Give it life. Make it real. To clarify your wishes, you might find it beneficial to answer the following questions. I suggest you respond to them twice—the first time without thinking at all, and the second time after reflection. On each occasion you do it, write down your answers. Then compare your sets of responses. Intuitive wisdom can come fast at some times and with space for reflection at others.

- *What do I most want, right now?*

- *At this time, what do I most need?*

- *What is my greatest gift?*

- *What is my biggest fear?*

- *What do I need to be happy, in this moment?*

- *What is my greatest obstacle?*

- *What is missing in my life?*

- *What am I most grateful for, right now?*

- *What is my mission?*

- *What fulfills me?*

- *What brings me joy?*

- *What about my life do I want to be different six months from now . . . a year from now . . . in two years?*

Many people find that writing a mission statement or creating a list of desires helps them grasp what they want. You might choose to do that. Some ideas to consider are listed below. Think about what you want in each of them. Which ones are most important to you, and why?

- Relationships
- Finances
- House and home
- Time
- Health
- Body
- Mind
- Spirit

- Sexuality
- Creativity
- Work
- Possessions
- Travel
- Entertainment
- Values
- Legacy

Once you've done these exercises, I suggest that you rank your wishes. Pick the top two or three as your primary focus for creating your heart's desire. And make them very concrete.

What do I mean when I tell you to make your wishes "concrete"? Well, for instance, if you want a loving relationship, write down everything that matters to you about the partner you wish for. Include things like values, appearance, characteristics, ways of being with others, and so on. If, instead of a love relationship, you ranked financial security very high, begin to envision what security actually looks like. What do you have? How do you feel? What do, and can, you do? Where are you? Paint a whole picture. Remember, your heart's desire has to be *very* focused in order for energy to be drawn to it. Exactly what do you want? And what *don't* you want?

I'm going to tell you a story to help you understand why I posed the last question: *what <u>don't</u> you want?*

Debbie came to me before her second marriage exploded, but she was already very unhappy. Zach, her second husband, was an extremely handsome, wealthy fellow; and she'd been drawn to his charisma, looks, and financial resources. Her first marriage had ended after her husband had an affair and lost his family business. So, Zach's sensuality, sexual interest in her, attentiveness, and financial stability had been very appealing. Being adored and provided for mattered a lot!

Debbie, of course, wanted a marriage grounded in honesty, reliability, and respect. She didn't want to replay the betrayal and devastation of her first one. But she hadn't made those "value" characteristics a focus when looking to repartner.

Zach had a reputation for being a player and a two-timer. She'd been told this several times by different friends. Although she'd raised her concerns with Zach before their marriage, he'd brushed them off. Rather than getting out, she'd plowed ahead. So her worries and doubts went underground.

Debbie came to me three weeks before her fourth wedding anniversary to try to understand why she was so miserable. Within six weeks of our first visit, Zach told her he wasn't in love with her anymore. He was in love with someone else and wanted a divorce.

Why am I telling you this story? What's the lesson here? Well, remember Debbie's intentions? She wanted attention, adoration, and financial security. That was what she focused on. But even more than that, she wanted a different kind of relationship than she'd had. Because she hadn't made honesty, reliability, and respect part of her intention, she ended up stepping into another trap. She made a bad choice of mate. She did the same thing she'd done before—and got the same results.

So, the first action I urge you to take in working with this chapter's teaching is: *Identify what you want and <u>don't</u> want!* Make your desires *very* focused. And keep adding more details to your descriptions—every time something else occurs to you. Don't assume anything or you may very well re-create exactly what you don't want! You may do just what Debbie, and many others, have done. In her case, she married "the same man" twice! But we've all replayed our dysfunctional dynamics over and over again. And it takes a heck of a lot of focus to create something totally different.

All right, I think you get the first point of this action lesson. You have to identify and choose what you really, really want . . . and beware of accepting what you want to avoid.

But, as I'm sure you realize, identifying and choosing what you want is just the beginning. You might, for instance, already be in a relationship you do want. But since your world exploded in betrayal, you couldn't have been doing everything necessary to live your dreams. You got yourself into this crisis *somehow*.

So, what are a few of the other things you need to do differently? What are the minute-to-minute and day-to-day pitfalls you must face and master? I'm going to give you a series of 25 suggestions, and examples of how to use some of them. The issues I'll be covering are among the most common ones I see in intimate relationships in my clinical practice. Most of what you'll be reading below applies to any relationship. So, while the focus in the wording is on "partnerships," the lessons are actually crucial to healthy functioning in every setting! Think about how these points relate to your experiences in your friendships, parenting activities, and workplace.

Remember, we're all set up by our past histories to expect and replay old dynamics, but if we want to experience different outcomes, we have to be extremely careful not to keep doing what we did. I'm sure you've gotten trapped in some of the patterns I'll be addressing below. Look for what you need to hear in the suggestion list I've created. Pick out, choose, and act on the recommendations that you need to adopt. (I've had to use all of them at times . . . you may, too!)

1. Don't be a fix-it person. Be a partner.

2. Don't let your worry about hurting someone's feelings keep you mum. That kind of silence always backfires!

3. Ask for what you want and need. No one can read your mind.

4. Beware of trying too hard to please. You stop being yourself when you do that.

5. Let go of the need to control or to micromanage. Your partner will resent it, and you'll burn out.

6. Give it time. Don't respond out of anger or hurt. Think through what you want to say before speaking.

7. Own what is yours. Don't criticize or blame others for your bad days or mistakes.

8. Apologize for your insensitivity, error, or nastiness if you've done something hurtful . . . even if the other person played a part.

9. Don't be too quick to give in or give up. But realize there is a time and a place for deferring or dropping it.

10. Stay in the present. Avoid future forecasting and worrying about what will happen.

11. Keep in mind that *all* relationships are work. Sometimes you'll want to blow your partner off, or blow it all up, even if you're living your heart's desire. Keep asking yourself: *Is it good enough?*

12. Trust your gut. Your intuitive wisdom never lies.

13. Let go. Avoid getting attached to any outcome. The tighter you hold on to your expectations, the more life you'll squeeze out of your relationships.

14. Be yourself. Always!

15. Whenever you find yourself questioning whether you belong with your life partner, ask yourself how you usually feel in his arms. Often that's all you really need to know. For instance, if the world falls away and you're regularly at peace, you probably belong together. If, on the other hand, you frequently don't want to be near him, it's probably time to establish some distance.

16. Don't expect any one person to meet all your needs. No one can!

17. Be reasonable and forgiving. Remember that everyone has bad days and falls short sometimes.

18. Be flexible about "give-and-take." Sometimes you'll need more from your partner, and sometimes he'll need more from *you*. When you both are needy and stressed, don't fight! Call for reinforcements!

19. Remind yourself that you'll both experience ancient pains, fears, and trust issues in your current relationship, but they may not be about what's happening *now*. You have a lot of traumatic history and patterns to reprogram. Discuss your feelings and experiences with one another to get clarity and perspective. (Talk to friends and therapists, too.) Banish blame. And check out what's really going on. Doing so will be very healing.

20. Rest easy. Sometimes you just need to sleep on it before you know what's bugging you or what you must do. Trust that you'll be given what you need, *exactly* when you need it!

21. Say "Thank you," "I love you," and "You're the best" whenever it occurs to you!

22. Do nice things for others, and let them know how much it means to you when they do nice things for *you*. It's very easy to take one another for granted.

23. Beware of attributing motivation to your partner's behavior. Don't assume you know why he did something. If his actions hurt you, ask him about his intention. Chances are that you're wrong in your assumption.

24. Make time for fun. All work and no play kills romance, friendship, and love! Schedule breaks, dates, and getaways.

25. Focus on what really matters. Don't sweat the small stuff . . . and most of what consumes our energy *is* the small stuff!

You've just read 25 suggestions that can help you manifest your heart's desire. If you follow them regularly, you'll be living your dream in no time. But what is actually involved in using these tools to stay out of old traps? Let's look at some examples.

Our first concerns numbers 2, 3, 4, 11, 14, 19, 23, and 24. We'll be revisiting the story of Dan and Alice. You may recall them from Chapter 1: Alice learned of Dan's affair during her phone call from hell. The couple had become my patients, and each had taken on years of self-examination and counseling to heal their marriage. I'd like to use their story to illustrate the role of old tapes and teachings in creating a dysfunctional relationship that included betrayal . . . and how 8 of the 25 principles you just read were involved in the rebirth of their marriage.

Dan and Alice met in high school. They were childhood sweethearts, each other's first loves, and crazy about one another. They were married and began having children while they were still practically kids themselves! Both were compliant, polite, very nice young adults from families where keeping the peace was considered a virtue. They learned: "If you don't have anything nice to say, don't say anything at all." Neither had ever seen their parents disagree or even negotiate differences. They had no idea of the work involved in making a relationship successful.

But viable relationships require a foundation of mutual respect, give-and-take, expressing needs to one another, and doing our best to be there for our partners. Disagreements are inevitable, and necessary, in forming a strong union. None of us can read someone else's mind, and we can't assume a lack of caring or concern for us when our unexpressed desires are ignored.

Dan came from a very large family. He was the baby of 12 children, and often an afterthought. He was to be seen and not heard, and he learned to fend for himself. Being a good boy is how he got by. He could be counted on. Dan rarely said no to any request. As an adult, he was constantly helping out his neighbors, friends, and even strangers. He was "other" focused; that is, he rarely considered his own needs, feelings, or desires. He'd learned they were unimportant and would get ignored, so he denied their existence. And he surely never asked his wife, or anyone else, for anything.

But he had needs that were unmet. He needed more affection. He needed to be drawn out and validated. He needed to be adored. He needed to be acknowledged for being a good provider.

Alice, by contrast, grew up in an emotionally unexpressive home where she learned to be a good homemaker. She never saw signs of physical affection between her parents. No one ever hugged her or said "I love you." She learned that love meant preparing meals, organizing the household, being physically present for your spouse and children, and making life work. Being a good wife entailed being grateful for your lot . . . even though you weren't to express that. And it surely never involved letting on that you were unhappy or yearned for more time with your husband.

Alice had needs that were unmet, too. She wanted more attention from Dan. She desperately wanted him to help *her* more and *strangers* a little less. She wanted him to fix and update his own home, take trips with her, and buy her flowers. She wanted to be seen, but never said so.

Both Dan and Alice were lonely, hurt, and frustrated in their marriage, but neither discussed it. So, when a woman whom Dan was helping out began to flatter him and became affectionate, he responded to her. He was longing for the contact . . . and he couldn't say no. Eventually, he got involved in an addictive affair. And his marriage exploded.

Much of my work with Dan and Alice involved practicing communication skills. Once I realized that for them it "wasn't nice" to ask for your needs to be met, we worked on why it was necessary to ask and how to do it. We kept clarifying the reasons why they'd gotten so disconnected and figuring out ways they could be really present to one another in the moment. We planned romantic time, paint-the-house time, and vacation time. We worked on values clarification and on how to say no without feeling guilty. And we looked at the motivation for their individual behavior. Each was quick to feel hurt by the other. They had a pattern of attributing motivation to one another and reacting to false assumptions.

As you know, it took years of work for Dan and Alice to heal their marriage. They were ultimately extremely successful. They're now "less nice," more grateful, and often joyful in their shared life.

Alice and Dan's story was a long example. Let's go through some briefer vignettes. Here's an illustration of a "fix-it person":

> Matilda came to me after being betrayed by a man who had created constant problems that she had routinely fixed. She was great at rescuing situations—tiny to huge. Whatever problem came her way, she solved. Since she couldn't count on the man in her life, she found a way to work around him.
>
> But Matilda was now seeing a new man. And, thankfully, she'd chosen a responsible, reliable one in George. Yet she was doing some of the same things with *him*. She was reminding George to make calls. She was cleaning up after him and making plans for the two of them without consulting him. In response, George was getting irritated. He'd say, "I've lived for 42 years without you. Don't you think I know how to take care of myself?"
>
> Matilda's work with me involved letting go of the need to fix what wasn't hers to handle anymore. She had to learn when she could let down her guard. She needed to allow George to do his part. She began to welcome his role, even if his way of handling things wasn't what she would have done. The letting go of *total* responsibility was scary, and ultimately, very liberating for Matilda!

The next example I'd like to share with you is a "biggie." We all get trapped in this one. It's about the importance of letting go of the need to be right. It's about apologizing and owning *our* parts even if the other person has hurt or wronged us, too!

Tina and Alex were in my office to process a fight they couldn't get past. As is often the case, they both wanted to tell their sides of the story so I could render a judgment as to who was at fault. But a focus on right and wrong kills relationships, so I don't do that.

What was the fight about? Tina was a recovering alcoholic, and she'd had to struggle a lot to stay sober. Up to the time of the emergency appointment, she'd been doing well for a long period, but she'd had a slip, and Alex was enraged with her.

Here's what transpired before our session: Tina had come clean about her lapse earlier in the day and let Alex know that she needed to attend an AA meeting that night. This was a lot of progress for Tina. Even so, Alex had begun screaming at her, "You don't care about me or our son! If you did, you wouldn't have drunk today. I'm tired of your lies and insensitivity. You'll never change!"

Tina had tried to respond to Alex . . . but nothing she said could make a difference. When they arrived in my office, both were hurting. Alex was feeling unloved and unable to trust his wife after so many years of struggle. Tina was feeling attacked and belittled when she'd been honest, direct, and responsible. Each felt wronged by the other and wanted validation.

I asked Tina to step into Alex's shoes. What might he be feeling behind his hurtful, attacking statements? And how might she have played a part in his pain? Tina softened as she began working this exercise. She understood that living with her and her disease for 13 years had taken a toll on Alex. While she was in a different place today, in the past she'd often been dishonest. And Alex had been regularly hurt, angry, and scared. Perhaps he'd just begun to believe the past was history. Maybe this episode had made him afraid about the future.

At my request, she checked out her ideas with Alex. Tears came to his eyes as he nodded to indicate that she was right. "I'm sorry for the pain I've caused you," she said. "I know it hasn't been easy living with me."

Alex didn't need me to encourage him to do the step-into-her-shoes exercise, because once Tina apologized to him, owning his part became easy. "It's only because I love you that I get so scared and angry. I'm sorry I said those mean things. I don't really believe them," he said. And as they hugged each other, I reiterated the lesson of suggestion number 8: We need to step into our partner's shoes and apologize for our insensitivities, errors, and hurtful behaviors . . . even if our partners have been hurtful to us, too. Making relationships be about right and wrong kills them!

I'll end this chapter with one more example. And it's a reminder to pay attention to point 25: *Focus on what really matters.*

Dahlia was in a new love relationship, and her birthday was coming up. She'd been with Justin for five months, but he hadn't mentioned anything about getting together or what they might do to celebrate her special day. She'd thrown him a birthday party the month before and invited 20 of his friends for beer, pizza, and cake. Yet her birthday was a week away . . . and he'd said nothing.

"What's his history around birthday celebrations?" I asked.

"Well, he could never please his ex-wife," she said. "And he told me birthdays are no big deal to him. I didn't need to do anything for his."

Since Dahlia approached birthdays differently, she'd gone to great lengths to give him a lovely day. She was angry. She was feeling uncared about. "It's about give-and-take. He's taking but not giving," she said. She took a deep breath. "Maybe I'm with the wrong guy."

"What do you most want for your birthday?" I asked.

And as Dahlia sat with the question, she realized that a romantic dinner with Justin and a birthday card was all her heart desired. I suggested she ask him if he would do these things for her. Perhaps she was creating unnecessary upset for herself.

By Dahlia's next therapy visit, her birthday had come and gone. She came into my office smiling. She'd had a lovely dinner with her new love and felt grateful for his presence in her life. "Boy, was I making a big deal out of nothing," she said. "It's so easy to lose sight of what's really important." And so it is!

Let's recap. You can have the life your heart desires, but you have to trust in your ability to create it, and you must take action after action to achieve it. Banish doubt, extinguish blame, and choose to step fully into your story. You can do it differently. You can manifest your dearest wishes one moment at a time! Use the tools in this chapter on a regular basis to see that happen. In the next one, you'll learn how to slow down, and understand and honor all of your involvements.

Chapter 8

SLOW DOWN: EXAMINE AND HONOR ALL OF YOUR INVOLVEMENTS

*H*ealing your life when your world explodes is a multi-stage process, and it can't be rushed. The fact that it takes a long time to recover can be very frustrating.

The unknown is scary—we all want to know what's going to happen, where we'll be, and how everything is going to "work out." When our universe shatters, we find ourselves adrift, lost at sea. Much of what had given our lives meaning, purpose, and direction has suddenly been tossed asunder. And we can't help but question who we are, where we are, what matters, and where we're going. We surely struggle with knowing whom and what we can trust, and we question whether we'll be okay in the end. So we want quick answers, and we can be driven to find them prematurely.

So far in this book, we've been focusing on what you need to learn from your history and betrayal experience. You've been learning how to create your heart's desire. I've reassured you that you'll get there and have given you tools and strategies you need, but I haven't talked much about the circuitous path you'll be taking from here to there.

It's time to get into that lesson. What *more* is actually involved in the process of rebuilding a shattered world?

You must slow down so that you can evaluate and honor all of your past involvements. You need to understand your prior feelings, behaviors, and choices in all areas of your life. Why is that? Well, living your dream involves salvaging and nurturing what you must grow, and shifting or letting go of involvements that no longer serve you well. You can only figure out which involvements are what when you come from a place of calm, peace, acceptance, openness, and presence in the moment. And you surely can't just "be" at the beginning of your betrayal experience. Initially, when your world explodes, you need all your energy to survive and cope from day to day.

But, thank heavens, nothing is forever. We human beings are highly resilient creatures, so as soon as we can move beyond our overwhelming pain and out of survival mode, we itch to start taking action. We want to heal. But there's a particular process involved in doing so. The lesson of this chapter—*slow down and honor all of your involvements*—has a place in that process. I'd like to describe it to you.

In my life and clinical practice, I've traveled the journey from betrayal to transformation many times. It regularly goes something like this:

- **First** comes the betrayal and devastation. Feelings, like the ones we covered in Chapter 1, are overwhelming and need to be addressed.

- **Second** comes the survey of damage and risk. A coping, surviving, and *How do I make it from day to day?* stage sets in. This can go on for a long time.

- The **third** stage involves taking steps in the direction of moving on and getting out, as well as fighting for and building a short-term future. This phase can also take many months to years.

- In the **fourth** stage, people begin to see light at the end of the tunnel. They start thinking more globally about what they want and how they got to where they are. They begin using that learning to create their hearts' desires.

But then there is a plateau—a "rest, regroup, revisit, and reevaluate" stage. This period comes after the crisis has passed, after the fear of survival has diminished, and once a new equilibrium has been established. At this point, individuals are able to engage in a deeper contemplation, questioning, and evaluation of past choices. They often remember or give voice to hurts long buried, minimized, or denied. They grieve, mourn, rage, and often forgive themselves for unknowingly stepping into, and staying in, traumatic situations. They own their mistakes. They find ways to accept and love themselves more fully. They begin to heal themselves at a deeper level.

They also start to examine the structure of their lives before betrayal and explore what makes sense now. This process of looking at our past involvements in order to design a more functional new structure involves dealing with what I call the "balance-counterbalance" issue. This concept can be very confusing to understand in the abstract. And, since this chapter's lesson is about stepping fully into your "rest, regroup, revisit, and reevaluate" stage, I'd like to give you an illustration of what is involved.

Mandy was the fix-it gal. She came from a family of five children and was the only girl. Her mom had been controlling, critical, and emotionally unengaged. Her dad had been happy-go-lucky outside the home, but had often skipped out on the household to avoid his wife's tirades. Mandy had taken on care of her mom, brothers, and dad. She had been the "fixer" for everyone.

She married a man, Al, who, unbeknownst to her, was manic-depressive. They had three children together before his illness took off to the point that he became dangerous to Mandy and her kids. In his manic psychotic states, Al would threaten their lives. When he began wielding knives and hurling them around, she came to me for help getting out.

First, we worked on how she could leave and keep herself and the children safe. Second, she figured out how to get divorced and provide for herself and the kids day to day. Third, she began examining how she got to such a place of trauma in her life and how to keep from repeating her family dynamic. Her parents were of great financial help in enabling her to move through the process.

Once Mandy was finally divorced, living in a different town from her ex and working part-time, she got to the "rest and regroup" stage. She began to realize that she hadn't really been present in her own story. Mandy discovered that she was burned-out. She didn't want to keep running so much.

As she slowed down and took a breather, she saw how much of her past life had been organized around her children. She'd been the president of a parent-teacher association for three years, a volunteer in each of her children's classrooms, the social director for many school events, the perfect homemaker, and a mom who would drop whatever she was doing to immediately attend to the tiniest request from any of her kids. She made every meal from scratch, too!

You might think, as Mandy did for a long time, that being a good mother means putting your kids first so much that *you* stop existing at all. My patient had learned to be that sort of parent and caretaker. And she'd gotten a lot of validation from it. She'd felt needed, appreciated, and emotionally engaged; she'd derived a sense of purpose and a feeling of connection; and she'd gotten enough good stuff from playing that role to keep herself going through many years of great challenge. Being a caretaker was actually part of what enabled her to survive!

But as Mandy began to settle into her new life, she realized that being a full-time caretaker to others was too exhausting. She couldn't keep giving from a dry well. She needed to replenish herself and establish a new balance between self-care and "other-care." She began to reflect: Maybe it was time to stop volunteering so much, to order pizza and takeout a few times a week, and to get herself a massage. Perhaps the old balance couldn't hold anymore and a new structure was necessary.

It took Mandy two years to create a new balance-counterbalance structure that worked. She needed to sort out how much of what she used to do she wanted to *keep* doing and how much she wanted to change. She kept checking in with her wise self through the process. *What does my heart desire right now?* she'd ask. The rebuilding process involved slowly stepping out of her volunteer roles until she was only doing occasional projects at the schools and chaperoning one or two class trips every few months. She hired a mother's helper, a teenager in her neighborhood, to share in transporting her children and preparing some meals; joined a book club and a singles' social group; and went back to school one night a week.

In her "slow down" phase of healing, Mandy found a new balance for herself that was the right fit and combination of activities. It took her several years of exploration, trial and error, and false starts to sort out what would work well enough for the current time. And it would continue to be a work in progress. Making over our lives always is! It involves learning to honor all our parts.

You see, no matter what your life looked like before your betrayal experience, all of your activities and choices balanced one another. You did what you did, to cope with what was. And it will take you a while to fully grasp your story. So, for example, you may have put in long hours at work partly to keep from being home . . . and also because you felt accomplished and connected there. Or you may have spent lots of time with friends, while household chores took a backseat because your mood would plummet without the social contact . . . and the connections felt good. Or you may have devoted a lot more time and money to your physical appearance than you now need to, because looking good back then fed your otherwise down-trodden sense of self-esteem. And so on.

I think you get the point. There is a good reason for everything you've done up until now. And thankfully, you were able to create a balance that served you well enough in many ways. But rebuilding means looking at every facet of your old structure. I urge you to lovingly let go of the beams you no longer need to hold you up, and to claim and fortify the trusses that will best "gird" your new edifice! Sorting out which parts go in which pile and how many of each you'll need takes time. Give yourself the gift of that time, please. *There's no rush!*

Let It Be

In order to help yourself slow down and stay calm through the process, I suggest you use the song "Let It Be" by the Beatles. I've found singing that refrain over and over again to be very calming, soothing, and healing for myself and for many of my patients. The words contain a very crucial lesson, and the act of singing actually activates endorphins, or feel-good chemicals, in the brain.

Whenever you find yourself worrying, forecasting the future, or searching for answers before the time is right to get them, try singing that song. I'm sure you remember it. It reminds us that there will be an answer and to let things be as they are. As the waves of "Let It Be" wash over you, your system will settle down. (Feel free to pick a different song if other music and lyrics speak to you.)

What Does It Mean to Slow Down?

You may be wondering how to slow down and regroup. What is this R & R phase, and how can you be sure to enter it? How do you move into *being* as opposed to just *doing* all of the time?

Well, post-betrayal, many of us get to a point where we actually don't want to *do* anything. Often women come into my office worried about this. They aren't their usual busy, active, engaged selves. They just want to relax, watch movies, read books, snuggle in bed with their pets, or hang out with friends. To many of us, this feels like *doing nothing.*

But in reality, healing our lives when our worlds explode and sorting out what really matters to us is actually about doing just this sort of "nothing." We need to follow our hearts, joy, bliss, and desires to do frivolous things. Our inner wisdom is guiding us toward activities that heal us—even though those activities may feel like hibernation, laziness, or avoidance for a while. There's a reason for everything. Just think about why caterpillars build cocoons!

I'd like to give you a list of some things you might choose to do during this slow-down-and-regroup phase. These ideas come from seeing what has healed many others at this time. Read through the list, and pick out those suggestions that speak to you. Use them as the fancy strikes you. Trust your inner guide to direct you to where you need to go. And add your own ideas to the list. Make it *really* long!

1. **Sleep until you wake up.** Don't set an alarm some mornings. Just let it be.

2. **Eat dessert first.** Eat whatever you wish, whenever your heart desires. If you want pancakes for dinner one day, have them. Or eat a slice of rich chocolate cake for breakfast or a salad at 10 P.M.

3. **Read trashy romance novels.** There's a reason that "trashy" romances have such an appeal. They're a great escape. They appeal to our imagination. They let us play at stepping into other worlds. And they give us great ideas!

4. **Watch a movie marathon.** Stay up late, or take a holiday day, and watch three movies in a row in your pajamas. Pick comedies, love stories, action films, or dramas that appeal to you.

5. **Go skinny-dipping.** Jump into a lake or pool with no clothes on once the moon is full and the sun has set. Enjoy the feel of the water against your skin and the beauty of your body in the moonlight.

6. Dance like no one is watching. Put on your favorite CD and dance around your bedroom. Or go to a club and shimmy the night away.

7. Clean your home. Get rid of stuff you no longer need. Give away what doesn't work, fit, or appeal to you anymore. Dump the excess baggage!

8. Nest. Buy new dishes or towels or new sheets and a bedspread. Choose something lively and vibrant or beautiful and soothing. Make your house *your* home.

9. Try a makeover. Get your makeup done and your hair cut and colored in a new way, or update your wardrobe. Have fun trying out new looks!

10. Pray. Offer thanks and ask for strength, wisdom, acceptance, and healing of self/others. Prayer changes lives. You may know that already, and perhaps you even pray sometimes. If this activity resonates for you, I suggest that you do it daily. Take a moment or two each morning or evening to offer thanks or ask for strength. Talk to God or your personal higher power. This communion with something larger than yourself will heal you.

11. Exercise, meditate, or do yoga or tai chi. Many people find that settling into their bodies in these ways connects them with what's healing in the universe. Find an activity that does that for you, and use it.

12. Spend time being present in nature. Commit to spending some time in the natural playground each week, and pay attention to the wonder of the scene and space. Notice the scent of a flower, the shape of a cloud, the pattern of leaves on a tree, or the sound of water rushing over smooth rocks in a stream. Be in nature—really *be* there . . . and be uplifted!

13. Paint, draw, sing, sculpt, garden, or write. These are, of course, all art forms, and for many people, something deeply spiritual happens when they enter the creative process. A bigger force takes over and expresses itself as the separation between artist and art disappears. The creator is elevated by this experience. If any form of art appeals to you, start puttering around with it. Perhaps you'll find something to do on a regular basis that heals, uplifts, and empowers you. If you do, use it!

14. Explore spiritual homes, religious institutions, or church meetings. Begin a regular ritual practice. You can't find your spiritual home if you don't go searching for it, and you won't feel connected to that community if you don't regularly engage in any of its ritual practices. So start visiting different churches, synagogues, ashrams, prayer groups, Bible-study classes, Quaker Meetings, or any other institutions that could be options for you.

15. Surround yourself with people who believe in you. You can't create your heart's desire if you're immersed in criticism, doubt, and negativity, so examine the company you keep. Work actively and aggressively to cultivate nurturing relationships, and avoid those that hold you back.

16. Join a group. Whenever people come together around shared interests, values, or needs, miracles happen. The immediate connection that results from having a common challenge or purpose is deeply healing. I've seen wonderful things occur when people join regular yoga or exercise classes, meditation groups, communities of worship, book clubs, or supportive gatherings (such as AA, OA, Weight Watchers, and bereavement groups). In fact, I could make a list of possible organizations for you to join that would fill an entire book! The number of psychotherapy and support groups alone is huge.

17. Care for a pet. How many times have you smiled upon seeing a cute puppy, a tiny kitten, or a foal struggling to stand for the first time? Do you feel better after petting a bunny or cuddling an affectionate dog? Would you rather buy a calendar with scenes of baby animals or of still-life paintings on each page? What feelings come up when you remember a beloved animal from your childhood?

Pets heal. Our ongoing relationships with these creatures augment our immune function, heighten our experiences of meaningfulness, and lengthen our lives.

18. Laugh. Read comics, go to funny movies, or get together with friends who keep you giggling. Laughter is good for the psyche . . . and for the soul.

You just read through a list of 18 R & R suggestions. I hope some made you laugh, some appealed to you, and lots touched you where you need to be healed. Use these ideas to slow down and be with yourself. Keep adding ideas to the list, and don't let *anything* seem too ridiculous.

What Matters?

I'd like to close this chapter with an exercise you can use to help you build a new life structure that reflects what matters to you. One way to get clarity about the fit between your heart's desire and your life choices is to make two lists. In the first, write down all the people, places, things, activities, and values that you hold dear. Rank them in order of importance to you, with number one being the most important, and so on.

Then make a list of all the ways you invest your energy and time. Think of a typical day, week, or month. How much time in a given period do you spend on each activity? List your involvements in order of energy spent, with number one being the most demanding, and so on.

In the ideal world, you'd be devoting the bulk of your energy or time to what's most important to you, and the numbers would line up between the two lists. If you find that your number one priority consumes the largest share of your time, your next concern the second-greatest amount of it, and so on, you're amazing . . . and well on your way to wholeness!

Most people, however, find the comparison of their two lists to be far from ideal. But take heart, because you can only start from where you are. And by discovering the mismatch in your lists, you've identified your problems. Such recognition and acceptance are the first steps in transforming your life.

Begin thinking about the mismatch between your two lists or about the disconnects you've noted between your essence and your life choices. You can actually fix some of the problems by simply identifying them and making a conscious choice to allocate your time differently. For instance, you may value your marriage more than your social life, but realize that you're spending more time hanging out with your work buddies than with your spouse. Simply cut down on activities with co-workers and plan more "couple time" into your week. This simple list-making and comparison tool can go a long way toward helping you create your heart's desire. It will allow you to invest your energy and time in what matters.

In healing your life when your world explodes, you'll eventually be able to slow down, rest, relax, and take stock. But your opportunity to honor all of your involvements and change the structure of your life can only come after your crisis and survival periods have passed, you've gotten out of danger, and you've begun to identify your heart's desires and taken some actions toward creating the life you really want. You'll probably find yourself engaged in this demolition-and-restructure phase for a long time.

And as you take risks and try new things, you'll benefit from carrying the lesson of this chapter with you. Remember to slow down, let it be, and recognize that everything has been there for a reason. Trust your gut and intuitive wisdom to show you what works, and what doesn't, for today. And nurture yourself with the 18 suggestions I've offered you here as well as the ones you've added to the list. In the next chapter, you'll learn the importance of trying new things and growing from *that* process.

Chapter 9

TAKE RISKS, TRY NEW THINGS . . .
AND PAY ATTENTION TO HOW YOU FEEL

*T*he lesson of this chapter concerns the importance of taking risks, trying new things, and paying attention to how you feel in the process. If you think about what we've covered so far, you'll realize that we've touched on this theme a lot already. You've been encouraged to take charge of your life, believe in your dreams, envision your heart's desires, take action, banish doubts, and examine all of your involvements. I've urged you to do things differently in order to achieve different outcomes. And I've given you many illustrations of how others have learned and changed over time.

But I haven't yet given you enough tools to help you negotiate the hurdles involved in changing. Healing your life when your world explodes requires you to be in an ongoing process of transformation. You have to do almost everything a little bit differently. You must take risks, try new things, and approach many *old* ones in novel ways. You have to work at tolerating the discomfort that comes from stepping into the unknown and become adept at allowing yourself to register how you feel in that process. You see, the only way out is *through!* In order to get out of your old patterns and into new, rewarding places, you've got to traverse a lot of unfamiliar terrain. And that can be scary.

Given that you've been burned, you're probably fearful of stepping out. You've been violated, deceived, and let down. You know that you want something better and that it's up to you to create it. But, like most of us, you're fearful of taking risks. You don't want to get more of the same, and you're concerned that you might.

I know that worrisome drill. I've lived it over and over again myself and have circled through it with many of my patients. What's familiar is comfortable . . . in a miserable sort of way. And doing every day differently can be overwhelming . . . to say the least. But, as the expression goes, nothing ventured, nothing gained. So let's have at it. Let's create the lives of our dreams.

I want to reassure you of something. Your inner wisdom, and the good counsel of friends and confidants, will be your guide. There is brilliance in your inner voice, your deep knowing, your intuitive self. While taking risks can be scary, you're not alone in the dark. If something feels really wrong in your gut, it is! And if something else keeps calling you to it, it's right for that moment. Remember that nothing is permanent. You can learn and change all the time. And so you will.

So what kind of risk taking am I talking about in this chapter? Well, I'll start with 16 suggestions. Each example encourages you to step out and do something that makes you vulnerable in a new way. Add your own ideas to this list:

1. Allow yourself to go out to dinner or to a movie alone.

2. Take the initiative to ask someone—male or female—to join you for a drink or on a hike.

3. Get a body piercing or tattoo.

4. Pursue a dormant interest or one you gave up on when *he* told you that it was frivolous.

5. Sign up for a class that interests you even if you have no knowledge of, or skill in, the subject matter.

6. Go on a singles' cruise.

7. Join a dating service, hiking club, or book group.

8. Train for a marathon or triathlon with others . . . even if you've never competed before.

9. Take a vacation to a place you've always wanted to go—alone, with your best girlfriends, or with people you don't even know.

10. Buy sexy clothes and allow yourself to wear them in public.

11. Volunteer for a challenging work assignment that you would have avoided in the past.

12. Interview for a job that speaks to you . . . but that wasn't "acceptable" before.

13. Date men with sex appeal even though they're not "marriage material."

14. Let friends and family members know what you want, need, fear, or are feeling.

15. Let people help you.

16. Ask for what you want and need.

Some of the suggestions you've just read may already be part of your routine, while others may be novel or kind of scary. Begin doing new things that challenge you—and old things with a new twist. As you take on this exercise, notice which activities you enjoy and which ones you don't. Discover parts of yourself that have been buried, and honor those bits that long for more expression. Don't expect new skills to come easily. Stay with your studio-art course or book club for a while. If you like something at all, give it a chance. Let yourself be a novice . . . and let yourself be surprised!

Getting the Love You Want

Trying new activities is one kind of risk you must take to heal your life. But there's another that is also part of this lesson. It's the relational one—that scarier, harder, "stick with it even when your old self wants to run away from it" one. Yes, you've been betrayed and burned. But you gotta let yourself be vulnerable again. You must open yourself up to new relationships. And in order to create your heart's desire, you have to behave differently in your relationships— every day.

This piece, getting the love we want, can be very difficult. The process can be torturous and gut-wrenching. We have to open ourselves up and ask for what we want and need. We have to share our feelings. But . . . it's scary. We make ourselves vulnerable to criticism, rejection, betrayal, or abandonment. We're powerfully driven by our longing for approval and stability, which starts in childhood as we seek positive reinforcement from our parents. That lesson—*be what others want or need you to be*—is firmly ingrained, and we can carry forward the dread of abandonment in profound ways. In some deep and primitive fashion, we may fear for our survival when we aren't accepted for who we are.

Additionally, the more we open ourselves up to others— the more we share our weak, sensitive, and vulnerable spots—the more likely we are to be hurt. Those who know us best can give the most support, but they can also injure us severely, attacking us in ways that wound and abandoning us both emotionally and physically. Whenever we step into intimacy, we invariably accept great joy and deep pain. They come together; we can't have one without the other.

As adults, we can survive and grow stronger each time we're hurt. In fact, our suffering can teach us about joy. We need the downs of life to recognize and appreciate the ups. And most people who love or have loved deeply say that the heartache is a small price to pay for the magic, wonder, and joy found in the bond with another.

But you're probably doubting your ability to be joyful in love. Your love life hasn't exactly given you what you've longed for, and you've experienced one pain heaped upon another until your whole world actually collapsed. You're probably wondering if it's safe to venture out into that arena again and questioning whether you can do it differently. Are there tools that can help you? Will you be able to spot and respond appropriately to potential danger? Will the universe deal kindly with you as you wobble around on your new and shaky legs?

Questions and doubts are likely filling your brain. That makes sense. It's "normal." But it's worth challenging yourself. My personal and clinical experience has taught me that you'll be rewarded for your efforts. I've been around this risk-taking-and-rebuilding process a lot of times.

I urge you to push yourself to be open. Use affirmations, visualizations, psychotherapy, prayer, and whatever else you need to empower yourself to take risks. Open your heart, mind, and soul to other human beings. Don't allow fear to limit, govern, or control you. Step into your life fully, wholly, and optimistically. Pay attention to how you feel. Honor your inner wisdom and the universe will support you in your endeavors.

I'd like to walk you through a series of communication skills and tools that can help you in your efforts to find the love you want. This type of guidance will make your risk taking easier! The skills we'll cover are:

1. Communicating your feelings respectfully

2. Setting boundaries

3. Expressing anger, hurt, or disappointment

4. Revealing your feelings in a safe way

5. Offering constructive criticism

6. Asking for help

7. Saying no without feeling guilty

8. Offering support without being overbearing

9. Apologizing when you fall short

Communicating Your Feelings Respectfully

How are you supposed to talk to other people? And what does it really mean to listen? What is healthy, effective communication; and have you been doing it? These are crucial questions. We often think that we're communicating when we're actually building walls and setting up barriers. We routinely judge, devalue, and criticize one another without even realizing what we're doing. We focus on other people instead of ourselves and usually tell them what they should do or what they're doing wrong. But the kind of sharing that fosters intimacy is accepting, supportive, respectful, humble, and most important, nonjudgmental.

In order to help you communicate more effectively, I want to give you a template to use when talking about yourself and working to connect with others.

Recite the following, inserting a statement of fact and a feeling word:

When you _____ [a], I feel _____ [b].

   a = a nonjudgmental statement of fact, such as "walk out of the room while I'm speaking"
   b = a feeling word or a description of an emotional state, such as "hurt" or "devalued"

Remember not to add *like, that,* or *as if* after the word *feel* in the above template. As soon as you do so, you shift the focus *away* from you and your feelings and *onto* the other person. You're then likely to say something critical.

You probably realize that when you make judgmental statements, you distance yourself from others. And when you share your pain, struggles, joys, and challenges with them, you foster empathy and connection. Making yourself vulnerable is a crucial step in getting the love you want in relationships, so use this tool on a regular basis. Become expert at sharing yourself to get what you most want and need.

Setting Boundaries

One of the most challenging issues we all face in relationships is how to set limits or boundaries without being hurtful, being critical of others, or feeling guilty or bad about ourselves.

While we all need one another, we require our personal space. We need downtime to be with our own thoughts. Of course we must distance ourselves from those who unsettle, hurt, or abuse us, but we also need distance from those we care about and enjoy. We must also remove ourselves from unsolicited advice, from help that feels intrusive, and from energy that's overbearing.

So, what's the best way for you to set limits or boundaries? The first step is to sort out what you feel and need. Your second step is to convey your needs without criticism, blame, or judgment. Validate yourself a lot. You owe it to yourself, and the other person, to honor your feelings and needs.

Beware of a common pitfall many of us trip over when we're expressing hurt, anger, or our need for space. We tend to push the other person away with blame or judgment. We do this when we start a sentence with one of the following phrases:

- *You never . . .*
- *You always . . .*
- *Why don't you . . .*
- *Why won't* [or *can't*] *you . . .*

Remember that respectful communication starts with "I feel" phrasing, so setting boundaries in a caring way means letting the other person know where we are emotionally and what we need.

I suggest you start practicing boundary-setting skills with the following two hypothetical scenarios. Write your thoughts about each of the questions posed in the text. Then read the option I offer. See what you learn as you go along.

1. Let's say you need time to think about something and aren't ready to talk about it just yet. What might you say?

    Here's one suggestion: "Nothing personal, but I need time to think about what happened. Could you give me some space? Perhaps we can talk about it later."

2. Or let's suppose you're feeling ambushed or derailed by the multiple questions your two children keep firing at you while you're trying to cook dinner. What could you say?

    How about: "Tracy and Sam, I'm really interested in what you have to say, but I can't concentrate on making dinner and talking to you at the same time. Please save your questions for a little while. I'll be able to talk with you when we're sitting together and having dinner."

Practice this skill with hypothetical situations and real-life examples. You can learn to set boundaries in a deeply honoring fashion and create fabulous relationships in the process.

Expressing Anger, Hurt, or Disappointment

Now it's time to learn how to avoid a common error we all make, mostly when we're hurt, angry, or disappointed. It involves attributing motivations to other people's behavior when we don't really know what's going on within them. Although we're often aware of what others have done to lead us to feel hurt, angry, or disappointed, we really don't know why they acted as they did. Yet we often assume we do!

Here are some examples of common scenarios:

- A friend arrives late for a lunch date. You feel hurt, angry, or disappointed, and think: *She doesn't care enough about me to be on time.*

- Your lover goes to the market and neglects to purchase the milk you requested. You feel hurt and angry. You tell yourself: *He's always thinking about himself. He's more concerned with getting what <u>he</u> wants than what I need.*

- Your birthday is coming up, and your family members haven't asked you how you want to celebrate. They begin scheduling activities for that date as if it's any other day. You feel hurt, angry, or disappointed; *you begin focusing on how thoughtless, inconsiderate, and nasty your relatives are!*

In the examples you just read, I attributed to you thoughts about the motivations of the other people involved—you "knew" what led them to act as they did, and your "knowing" fed your distress. But in real life, you wouldn't really be certain why your friend was late for lunch, why your boyfriend forgot the milk, and why your family wasn't acknowledging your upcoming birthday. And if you began acting or speaking from your place of assumption, you'd create all sorts of tension, upset, and strife. And no doubt your hurt, anger, and disappointment would grow.

But there's an alternative way to honor your feelings and respect the other person in each scenario. Just think about it. Imagine other motivations for their behavior. What if your friend was in a car accident en route to lunch, she briefly lost her car keys on the way out the door, or—even more embarrassing—*you* had written down the wrong time for the lunch in your date book, and she was actually on time?

Or imagine that your boyfriend bought the requested item at the market and the bagger failed to pack it into the cart. And in our final scenario, what if your family members were neglecting to acknowledge your upcoming birthday because none of them wanted to mess up and spill the beans about the huge surprise party they were planning?

I'm sure you realize that these reasons for what happened in the scenarios described are just as likely to be the case as the motivations I initially had you create in your mind. But we rarely give one another enough of the benefit of the doubt. We jump to hurtful conclusions and create a lot of pain as a result. So what is the best way to think and communicate when you're hurt, angry, or disappointed?

When you're feeling these emotions, take care to use your template for healthy communication. Remember: *When you* _____ *, I feel* _____ . Be sure to avoid assumptions. Don't attribute motivation. In fact, it's best to *ask* about the reason for someone's behavior. You may very well be surprised!

Practice expressing hurt, anger, and disappointment without attributing motivation, passing judgment, or casting blame. You'll get the most out of this exercise if you create responses to actual hurts you've experienced in your daily life. Try sharing your sentences with your friends and relatives. See which statements feel and work best. The most effective ones bring you closer to those you care about— although you may all experience pain and anxiety in the communication process.

Revealing Your Feelings in a Safe Way

You've learned a lot about how to honor your feelings and how to express them respectfully. You've also learned that some relationships are more healing, while others are more self-destructive. You've lived this lesson in many ways. You know about the importance of building healthy connections and avoiding involvements that feel toxic.

But even in the best of relationships, it isn't necessarily safe (or healthy) to divulge all of your feelings all of the time. So how are you to know what to share, and with whom? This is a very challenging question, as it concerns a very evolved aspect of self-care.

But you have the ability to sort out the answer! Your wise self, your intuitive wisdom, your gut sense is your guide . . . because, you see, you know where and when you feel at ease and when you feel unsettled. And I want to encourage you to tune in to your inner healer. Trust yourself. When you find yourself wanting to be open with someone, go for it—but only share a tiny bit at a time. See if you feel safe enough, and interested enough, to disclose a bit more. Always start by revealing feelings that don't seem especially scary. And hold the most private, vulnerable parts of yourself in a secluded, safe place until you know—for sure—that you're ready to bring them forth.

I suggest you use this strategy as you're getting to know new people. But don't stop there. Allow it to guide you in your most intimate and long-standing relationships as well. Keep checking in with yourself, because it's not safe to be completely open to anyone all the time.

If others try to push you to share more than you're ready to put forth, they're dangerous. Set limits and boundaries. If the pushy person won't back down or refuses to honor your need for space, it's unsafe for you to stay in the involvement. Seek whatever help you need to get out. Remember that healthy relationships are mutually respectful, interdependent but not codependent, and life enhancing. You feel comfortable being in them. And in healthy enough relationships, your need for safety will always be honored and respected. If it isn't, don't disclose. Get out!

Offering Constructive Criticism

None of us likes to receive unsolicited advice, and most of us feel put down when others offer us what they consider to be constructive criticism or feedback. Often they're telling us what we did wrong and what we need to change.

Most people find constructive feedback that is self-revealing to be easier to take than authoritarian or judgmental statements. Remember the difference between "I" and "You" statements. The former are easier for us to accept. And the more we share from an "I" place, the easier it is for others to hear us as well.

So, imagine the scenario: Your spouse is yelling at your daughter. She's yelling back and crying because she's overwhelmed by her "hard" homework. The scene is upsetting to watch. What could you say? Think of a self-revealing statement that is constructive. Write it down, and then read the following option I offer.

You might say, "I relate to your upset and anger. And I've tried yelling, too, but I find it works better when I ask our daughter if she needs help with her homework. I'm unsuccessful when I yell at her for refusing to cooperate. Perhaps you would benefit from trying what works for me."

Since it's so challenging to offer feedback constructively, you might be wondering *why* you should do it. Wouldn't it be easier to avoid the topic altogether? Well, the reality is that part of caring for one another—and partnering in life—means finding respectful ways to help each other grow. So there are times when we ought to offer feedback—to those potential recipients who are willing to hear it. And I urge you to practice sorting out who they are.

So the structure I suggest you use is (feel free to substitute your own words):

1. "I notice that _____ [a]."
   a = describe the behavior

2. Find a way to validate and empathize—for example, "I understand what you're trying to do," or "I've done that, too."

3. "I have found that when I _____ [b], I have more success."
   b = offer an alternative approach

Perhaps you'd like to try my approach. Again, I suggest you work on creating constructive-criticism dialogue. Use real-life situations, and then practice speaking your truth to those who matter. Pay attention to what language goes over easy and what needs to shift. Allow yourself to learn from your feelings on the receiving end of feedback, too. Getting the love you want in relationships means giving *and* receiving respectful feedback.

Asking for Help

It's hard for many of us to ask for help. We seem to believe we ought to be able to do it all alone; or we doubt we're worthy of, or entitled to, assistance. None of us can make it by ourselves.

So how are you to ask for help? The clearer you can be about your feelings and needs, the more effective you'll be in asking for what you require . . . and receiving it. And keep in mind that *needing is not the same as being needy.* You have great strengths. *You are not a victim.* Don't ever let yourself start thinking that you are. You're powerful and human!

We all need help, guidance, support, direction, and assistance at times. And it's your job to figure out what *you* need so you can be sure to get it. Be at least as generous toward others as you wish them to be toward you. No one will want to support you if you're unwilling to reciprocate. Getting what you need means giving, too.

But *how* are you to ask for help? Here are some principles:

- Be honest, direct, and clear.
- Avoid guilt-provoking statements.
- Minimize expectations.
- Respect the needs of the person you're asking.
- Let those you ask know you appreciate their willingness to consider your request.
- And, of course, thank anyone who offers to help you.

Here are a couple of examples of clear, specific, respectful requests for help:

- "I have a work obligation that prevents me from being able to pick up my son after wrestling. Would you be willing to bring him home tomorrow? I'll be glad to return the favor by picking up your son some other time."

- "I'm going through a challenging time right now and am wondering if you have an hour or two available to visit with me. You are such a wise and dear friend, and I would really appreciate your support and feedback. Is that something you can manage?"

I suggest you take a personal inventory of your needs and wants. Do you ask for help often enough? Too much? Could you do better? People *need* people—and you surely do. Respectfully, ask for what you need. You will be answered.

Saying No Without Feeling Guilty

Before we get to this next lesson, we need to talk about a crucial challenge many of us face in self-care when asked to do things by others.

Most of us have a tendency to take on other people's urgency as our own. We feel pressured to respond immediately. Yet when we answer quickly, we tend to say things we regret. We neglect to check with our inner guides. But we rarely even recognize the importance of creating that sort of space for ourselves. When a question comes up, we say yes . . . even if it means we're agreeing to take on more than is realistic or healthy.

So, on your way to saying no without feeling guilty, I want you to practice saying: "Let me think about it, and I'll get back to you." Begin imagining scenarios that you've already lived through in which you agreed to do something when asked . . . and regretted it. Now visually replay the scenario. Only, when the question comes this time, say something that buys you time to reflect. Connect with your inner voice, and then respond. Notice how you feel. After replaying a scenario with space for reflection, most people experience a sense of lightening, freedom, relief, or liberation.

When we've created space, it's much easier to find our personal best answers—and to become comfortable with "no" when that's the right response. We can think through why "no" is necessary. And we can even come up with caring, loving, and sensitive ways to express this sentiment. The more "no" feels right, the easier it is to say it without feeling guilty.

Offering Support Without Being Overbearing

Caring about one another in relationships involves offering and extending support to those we love. But there's often a fine line between what feels supportive and what feels controlling, overbearing, or intrusive. How can you tell the difference?

Each one of us has a different set point, a different boundary line, when it comes to experiencing an involvement as being helpful or controlling. So the best way to find out what works for those you care about is to ask them, but there's something you need to do first.

Before extending yourself, look at your own motivation. Ask yourself: *Am I trying to help in the way my friend wants to be supported; or am I trying to impose my will, my ideas, or myself? Am I trying to control the outcome; or am I simply here to serve, help, love, and care?* If you're not pure in your motivation, you'll be overbearing—and it will backfire. But even if you have the best of intentions, you'll mess up sometimes. You'll offer what *you* would want or need, when your friend may want or need something else. So I suggest you offer the help that makes sense to you, but ask if something else would be preferable.

Here's an example: Your friend Sam's parent has just died. You were in the same position the year before and felt supported when your friends called every day to talk, so you dial up Sam and say, "I'm so sorry about your loss. Would you like to talk?"

Well, as it turns out, Sam isn't a talker and hates the telephone. But he'd love some company! Being an expert at asking for what he needs, your friend says: "I so appreciate your call, and I'm glad you asked. I'd rather not talk, but I would like it if you'd come by and hang out for a while. We could play cards or watch a movie. I just need some company."

You'd probably feel grateful for Sam's honesty, since you want to help and he's telling you how to go about it. And, in response, you'd probably do your best to visit your pal as soon as you could.

If you're pure of heart and anxious to support your friends, you'll feel grateful when they tell you what they need. Even though you may not always be able to give them what they request, you can surely meet them halfway. And give-and-take is what healthy relationships are all about. So ask and offer . . . offer and ask . . . your way to getting the love you want!

Apologizing When You Fall Short

Why is it that you don't always feel better when someone apologizes to you? Have you ever noticed what makes some apologies feel sincere and other ones unreal or even hurtful?

A sincere apology is an "I" statement about an "I" action. It's followed by some desire to fix the hurt. Here is an example:

Jacob didn't leave work with enough time to get to his wife Sally's tennis match. When he arrived, she was very hurt and angry. He said, "I'm sorry to have caused you such pain by missing your tennis match. I love you, and I treated you badly. There is no excuse for my behavior. Is there anything I can do to make it better?"

Imagine yourself as Sally in the situation. While you may not feel totally better after hearing Jacob's apology, you would probably feel seen, acknowledged, and somewhat cared about. Contrast that with this "apology" by Jacob: "I'm sorry you're so upset. There was a lot of traffic today on the way home, and it took me longer than I expected to get here. How did your match go?"

On the receiving end of that "apology," you'd probably feel hurt and angry. Jacob isn't apologizing for anything he did! He's sorry *you* are upset, but he isn't owning his actions. On top of that, he's justifying his lateness without taking responsibility for his poor planning and insensitivity. Finally, he hasn't validated your feelings or empathized with you. He hasn't offered to fix the hurt. And he's shifted the topic of conversation. He wants you to tell him how things went. That "apology" is a *non*-apology! It's an inflammatory series of sentences that foster upset.

Take note: A real apology follows the template for communication you've already learned. It's an honest, caring

"I feel" statement about an "I did" sort of behavior. The concerned apology is: "I feel sorry for missing your tennis match." By contrast, whenever your "I feel sorry" is followed by a "you" phrase, it's an unproductive, uncaring, and often unnecessarily hurtful statement. Here is an example: "I feel sorry you're so upset." That statement pushes people farther apart. It adds insult to injury. And it surely doesn't get you any closer to self-empowerment or the love you want.

So, practice apologizing from a healthy, caring, and responsible place. Don't beat up on yourself when you mess up. We all do that. And we hurt one another without meaning to do so. But we're not doomed. We can triumph and connect. We're able to grow ourselves and our relationships every day. We're capable of learning from our mistakes. We *can* find joy, fulfillment, and love—one step at a time.

Common Dating Pitfalls

Okay! Now let's take a look at a series of common pitfalls that come up for many women in their efforts to create new romantic relationships. I've lived some of these, and I'm sure you have, too! And a number of them are outlined beautifully in the best-selling book *He's Just Not That Into You,* by Greg Behrendt and Liz Tuccillo.

Many of us women are regularly driven to make excuses for the men in our lives. We doubt in our own beauty, desirability, appeal, and fabulous natures. So, when the cute guy we've begun to date or are living with—or even married to—begins to disrespect us, we explain away the obvious. We don't trust our inner goddesses. Rather than allowing ourselves to recognize his lack of commitment to us for what it is, cutting our losses, and moving on to better things, we keep excusing him and hoping he'll change. *But we don't need to do that.* We deserve, and can create, our hearts' desires.

So what are some of these common misconceptions? What keeps us "in" with men who aren't "into" *us?* Well, we tell ourselves falsehoods such as the following:

1. He's too busy to call.

2. He doesn't want to date because it will ruin our friendship.

3. He doesn't really mean it when he says he doesn't want a serious relationship.

4. He's not being sexual with me because he's afraid of getting hurt again.

5. He's such a good catch even if I can't count on him to call; his disappearing act is okay.

6. He'll leave his wife, girlfriend, or lover for me.

7. He loves me even though he's mean, hurtful, and irresponsible.

8. I can't do better than him! I need to make it work.

9. I can't live without him even though I'm not happy *with* him.

10. I'm too needy—he's the best . . . even when he's really not that great.

Why might you fall into the trap of pitfalls like the ten you've just read? Your old tapes, big fears, and battered self-esteem propel you. And taking risks is scary. It's easier to doubt in yourself and in what's possible. You have a tendency to silence your heart's desires and replay old stuff.

Consider what negative affirmations keep you in relationships that hold you back. Add your stuck-in-the-mud statements to the list. And then blow the bullshit out of the water!

If you need reinforcement to stay out of sand traps like the ones I've just listed, read *He's Just Not That Into You*. It's empowering, clarifying, and affirming of your wondrous potential! Get out of what doesn't work . . . and allow yourself to work at what *can*.

I urge you to allow yourself to take risks. Use the communication tools you've learned in this chapter to make what's new and scary a little bit easier. Trust that if you honor the wisdom of your inner voice, you'll be healed. You can do this! Start with one scary step at a time, and keep on going. In the next chapter, you'll learn how to let your female friends help you as you travel your amazing journey of growth!

Chapter 10

LET YOUR FEMALE FRIENDS HELP YOU

One of the most crucial lessons I've learned from my betrayal experience is the importance of letting our female friends help us. Women heal women. We offer one another a kind of support that men can't give us. Our chromosomes, brain structure, neurochemistry, and hormones make for significant gender differences that are fundamental.

Our husbands, boyfriends, lovers, and male pals can't be our best friends. Our best friends and confidantes must be women like ourselves. The men in our lives might even be our soul mates—our partners in matches made in heaven. But they're not the same as we are. Men can't travel the relational, conversational, "emotionally attuned for hours" paths that women regularly walk. Their brains aren't structured to make that kind of caring and sharing possible. They don't really "get" us; and they don't know how to help us process what we need to feel, discuss, and emotionally resolve.

You'll learn more about what men can and can't do for you in the next chapter. But I've given you this preview of coming attractions that you've just read so you'll understand that you need to cultivate and allow your female friendships to heal your life. In this chapter, you'll be learning why and how to do that.

Why Women?

Women are emotional beings. We *feel* lots of stuff all the time, and we're extremely relational. We have feelings for and about others constantly. We're usually in touch with ourselves, whether we're happy, sad, anxious, excited, cautious, concerned, angry, or confused. We can usually figure out *when* something is bothering us and *what* it is, but we often need to think and talk about our feelings to get the clarity we do get—we need to hear ourselves process our experiences in order to understand them. We must be heard, seen, validated, and supported in our journeys toward self-discovery. And we require the input of others to keep us on track when we start doubting ourselves or what's possible. We just "need to talk," and spending hours connecting with one another on the phone or over coffee heals us!

When your world explodes in betrayal, you need to connect! You need to share your trauma, your pain, your fear, and the details of what you've lived through and are facing. You require the validation of others. You have to know that you're not alone, that what you're going through is awful, that you can be helped, and that there's light at the end of the tunnel.

Your women friends can hold your hand through this challenging period. As you talk to them, you'll hear yourself tell your story; and in the recounting, you'll make the unfathomable real. As your friends ask questions and express their dismay, shock, horror, and sadness, you'll gain perspective you don't yet have. You'll begin to recognize the intensity of hurt, pain, and devastation you've tolerated and lived with— perhaps for a very long time. You'll be offered guidance and help. Friends will direct you to good lawyers, doctors, therapists, and financial advisors, as well as other friends of *theirs* who have lived through similar challenges.

Your female allies will sit with you when it's too hard to be alone, watch your kids when you need to meet with a lawyer or get a massage, and offer to cook you dinner or take you to a movie. They'll help you see who you are—separate from him. They'll tell you the things they think about you and about him that they've never before shared. They'll validate your gifts and talents and point out *his* shortcomings. They'll let you know, in no uncertain terms, that you deserve and can have much more.

And that's just the beginning. Your female friends will walk the long journey to healing with you. They'll listen to you, support you, and help you through every step. They'll encourage you to try new things. They'll guide you through the difficult risks and self-changing acts that you take on. They'll help you figure out when you're doing old stuff and when you're actually making progress. They'll show you how to write a profile for an online dating service and lend you an ear as you describe one dating challenge after another. They'll hold your hand when you're hurt by yet another guy, and they'll fix you up with their friends.

You see, women are helpers, caretakers, and best friends. And we feel better when we're helping one another. Our relational connections heal us. We feel good when we aid our friends, and we all know *we* could be on the opposite side of the helping exchange the next time around.

Let's look at some examples of the roles women play in healing one another. I'll start with my own story.

Soon after my life exploded in betrayal, I was sharing some of the details of my experience with my friend Carol. She was horrified to hear what I'd been through and was also struck by how long I'd stayed in an awful marriage. Her reaction helped me see how much of myself I'd pushed underground to keep on going, and how prone I was to accept the absolutely unacceptable. When I said something about hoping Peter and I would be "friends" someday, she set me straight: "You will never be friends with him. He's not your friend." And, boy, did I get it! She was totally right. In those early weeks following my betrayal experience, I was still in fix-it mode. I was doing ingrained stuff that made no sense given the reality of what was. And my friends helped me "get real."

Today, when I think about what Carol said to me that day, I thank God she was so blunt. I was extremely stuck in dysfunctional thinking, and I didn't even realize it. During that conversation, she also told me, in just a few very powerful words, that my marriage was in no way how it was supposed to be. She said that I'd experience something totally different down the road . . . and she couldn't have been more prophetic had she tried to be! My new love, Tom, is nothing at all like Peter. And I've never been happier in a romantic relationship.

My conversations with friends like Carol in those early weeks and months taught me something extremely valuable, and I want to share that crucial lesson with you. During my many unhappy years of marriage, I kept *way* too much to myself. I regularly talked to my husband about my needs and unhappiness as if he were my best friend. And I talked to my parents. But I didn't talk to my girlfriends about the "private" stuff. I believed that I shouldn't share those things as long as I was trying to make my marriage work. As a result, I kept way too much of what I should have told my friends to myself.

Why do I say "should have told"? Because I know today that had I shared enough of the details of what I was going through in my marriage with trusted confidantes, I would have left sooner. I would have gotten the clarity, support, and perspective that I needed to move on. I would have saved myself a lot of pain and heartache. I was never going to live my heart's desire with Peter. When I was with him, I was actually miserable, stressed, and overwhelmed for years. And the handwriting was on the wall from the very beginning. I just couldn't read it alone.

Women buy tons of self-help books, seek counseling and guidance 80 times more often than men, and welcome one another in loving acceptance. Yet we martyr ourselves too much; keep our hurts, pains, and challenges a secret; and try too hard to make the unworkable work. We need to change! One of the most important lessons I've learned from immersing myself in the literature of addiction recovery is: *we are only as sick as our secrets*. And my personal life and clinical work have shown me how relevant those words are to relationship challenges. Don't keep your doubts, hurts, and pains a secret. Let other women help you. Pick safe friends as confidantes—and talk to them. Ask them to help you, and let them in.

I'd like to share another story with you to illustrate the role women can play in healing one another. This one concerns a lady named Andrea who came to me six years into a problematic marriage.

Andrea had first heard me speak at an integrative-health talk for women, and having been through a series of significant health challenges of her own, she wanted to do everything she could to prevent further problems. Recognizing that stress can impair immune function, and living in a tension-filled marriage, she called me for a consultation.

During her initial visit with me, Andrea shared this concern: "I've been in two bad marriages already, and I'm really unsettled in this one. I got sick two years after marrying André, and it took me over three years to get well again. I'm afraid the stress I'm under in my marriage will make me sick once more, and I'm not sure what to do about it."

Andrea and I embarked on an extensive exploratory journey. She needed to talk so that she could make sense of her experiences. Without this kind of processing, she couldn't know what to do next, so I took her on as a long-term patient.

Over time, Andrea tried to describe the scenes that she was living through at home. She had to determine whether her marriage was making her ill and what, if anything, she could do to fix it. Yet, each time Andrea began to talk, she drew a blank at a certain juncture. She couldn't remember the details of any disagreement with André.

As she attempted to share the discussions she and her husband were having with one another, her body language spoke to me. She closed up, hugged herself, looked down, and turned away. When I pointed this pattern out to her, she told me she was doing exactly the same things in my office that she did in André's company. Almost invariably, when she spoke to him, she'd get overwhelmed and confused, and then she'd withdraw.

I told Andrea that I sensed she was afraid of her husband. I explained that I was concerned that she was so cowed by André's words and their delivery that she was becoming flooded with fear and worry in his presence. Then, in her hyper-aroused and anxious state, she wasn't able to think, talk, interact, or process. She was shutting down to get away! I wondered whether it was safe for her to talk to him at all.

As Andrea registered my feedback, she began to realize how on-target it was. She didn't feel safe with André. And she wasn't sure she *ever* had. He was an extremely scary guy, and some of her female friends had tried to get her to see that about him when they first began dating. She just hadn't let their words sink in. She'd so wanted to be loved and desired that she hadn't let her female friends help her enough. . . . But that was about to change.

As Andrea and I continued our sessions, I explained that her self-protective responses were there for a reason. It was important that she allow herself to honor them. She needn't push herself to connect when she was driven to withdraw. She could reach out to friends and me for support. She could set limits with her angry, controlling, and critical husband. And she could be safe. In fact, she would eventually gain enough personal clarity and strength to do what her emotional, physical, and spiritual well-being most required.

It took Andrea about a year of therapy to decide to end her marriage. During that period, she spent hundreds of hours talking with friends, journaling, and processing her experiences. She got support and guidance. The women in her life taught her to be gentle and patient with herself, which buoyed her. Eventually, she was able to tell André to leave. And following his departure, she learned enough about him to enable her to recognize how wise her inner healer had been in being scared. She discovered that André truly *was* dangerous!

Today, Andrea welcomes the support of her female friends in her life. She knows that her wise self and the loving support of trustworthy female friends will keep her from stepping into another lion's den. She's currently dating safe, respectful men; and she has empowered all her female friends to share their perspectives with her. She'll listen to them this time. As a result, she feels a lot safer!

The examples you've just read demonstrate how we women can support one another in processing our past histories, getting through crises, and moving out of danger. Now, let's delve into how our friends can help us rebuild our lives. I'll use my story again to demonstrate how much we women need to let our female friends help us heal. We can't do the whole thing alone! And stories can make this point real.

When my life exploded, I was a mess. I had no idea what sexually transmitted diseases I needed to be checked for or which tests I ought to have done. I needed to know details— the best- and worst-case scenarios. And I was scared! Even though I'm a medical doctor, it's been many years since I've treated patients for gynecological issues. So I reached out. I called my dear ob-gyn friend Debbie, whom I've known and loved for 28 years. She held my hand through that whole assessment process—even though we live 2,000 miles away from one another and are separated by three time zones! Debbie urged me to call her as often as I needed. And I took her up on her offer numerous times. She helped me through countless days of fear, and I'm grateful to be able to tell you that I'm healthy and unscathed today.

When my life exploded, I faced another challenge: my ex-husband stepped out of his historical participation in the financial obligations of our family. I had no idea how to provide for some of my children's pressing needs, so I turned to my women friends for direction, and among them Amy became another angel in my life. She sat with me for hours in Starbucks listening, empathizing, questioning, and guiding me through shark-infested waters. And she lent my son a car for eight months so he could get to school and to his sports and extracurricular activities! She helped me help him out until I could buy him a used car myself.

Amy is still cheering me on and validating my relationship and financial instincts. I solicit her feedback about the things she knows how to approach. It helps me to hear if I'm on the right track or not. That sort of clarifying input will help you, too! You can't do it all alone. Let other women in!

Learning about Men from Women

Many of my female friends have helped and continue to help me learn, grow, and heal my life. And I'm grateful to all of them. But I've been *most* helped by my dear friend Ann Marie. She is absolutely the one who has taught me what I needed to know in order to negotiate the challenges involved in building a new romantic relationship. Without her I wouldn't have ever understood the fundamental differences between men and women that underlie the lessons of this chapter and the next. Ann Marie helped me appreciate the push-pull nature of an evolving and developing love life. And without her input, I wouldn't have been able to tell for sure whether I was growing in a new romance or replaying my old dysfunctional patterns with a different love.

Ann Marie taught me that women heal women. Although I might have known that fact already, what I hadn't ever really understood is that men can't do it! Women hold each other in ways that *they* can't. Women are nurturers. Men are action figures! And when men feel emotional intensity or have a sense that we do, they often need to go away. They tend to feel overwhelmed by strong feelings and have to create space to find themselves. While we discover ourselves in sharing our emotional worlds with other women, men find themselves best in solitude and distance.

Men have a propensity for feeling engulfed or overwhelmed when they're in emotionally intense situations, so creating healthy romantic relationships with them will include periods of strong connection punctuated by periods of distance or space. And the more passionate your man is, the more intensely he'll connect to you and the more powerfully he'll insist on his need for distance. As a result, he could push you away in ways that may be very painful to you. Getting deeply involved with you will scare him to death, so he may "bust out" on a regular basis—for a while! He may even ask you to marry him and then tell you the next week that it's over or he needs to be alone. He may play this pattern out a number of times before he recognizes his ongoing comfort level with you. Men are funny creatures. And we women need one another to help us deal with their capricious natures.

When I met Tom, I called Ann Marie and said, "I need your help. Will you tell me when I sound sane and set me straight if I ever seem to be doing sick, old stuff? I really messed up before, and I don't want to make another mistake."

Ann Marie said I could call her anytime. And I even went to her home at midnight on one occasion . . . I was a wreck, and she helped me process my current relational challenge. Interestingly, Ann Marie told me that she learned something crucial from me about our needs as women. When I told her I needed her help, she learned that it was okay for *her* to ask for help! Because—surprise, surprise—she wasn't really comfortable allowing herself to do that either. So now I'm helping her with *her* stuff, and she's helping me with mine.

What sort of challenges has Ann Marie walked me through? Well, she taught me not to fear a man's withdrawal, as well as the importance of approaching him from my place of radiance—not need. When I'm most needy, he'll be most overwhelmed. I've learned to have much more patience with my man and myself. I allow myself to call Ann Marie when I get confused, anxious, or extremely unsettled. She's healed me by teaching me that women feel the pain of separation *whenever* their men need space, and this pain is *normal* for us. Having it doesn't mean we're cuckoo or enmeshed. It means we're women! And men don't feel this way. They feel differently!

Ann Marie has empathized and said, "It sucks. When you most need him, *he* needs distance." And she's helped me distinguish between my desire to have answers about the future and my true love and passionate feelings for Tom. She's told me that men's brains take about a year to catch up emotionally to what their words express. So in new love relationships, it may take men at least a year to be able to commit fully—even if they say something different about their thoughts, feelings, and desires early on. Ann Marie has helped me see that what women have to watch for is whether men are making shifts and changes in the direction of *their* expressed commitment. If so, we women must help each other be patient with the process. It's not going to be a straight line. We must expect the push-pull dynamic to go on for *at least* a year! And that's fast!

Remember that *Sex in the City* movie? The "wedding that wasn't" followed years of a shared life between a man and woman who were crazy about one another. Yet Mr. Big did that "man thing": he freaked out, briefly, on the way to the altar. And Carrie did that "woman thing": she went into total devastation mode, catastrophizing about his withdrawal. And both of them, as a result, experienced a lot of unnecessary heartache.

Trust me when I tell you this. New love in your life? He will wobble. It's in his masculine nature. And you'll worry, ache, and maybe even freak out. It's in your feminine nature. Let your female friends help you stay calm, clear, and collected through your healing journey. They'll be a great comfort for you. If and when you choose to cultivate love and romance again, draw on your friendships for support. Even if building a new love life isn't what's on your agenda right now, let your friends help you negotiate whatever you choose to take on.

Remember, women heal women! And men can't heal us. In the next chapter, you'll learn what men *do* have to offer and what they *can't* do for you. Whenever you're ready for that one, read the next page!

Chapter 11

LEARN WHAT MEN HAVE TO OFFER
AND WHAT THEY CANNOT DO FOR YOU

*O*n the last chapter, you got a preview of this one. As you were learning about the importance of letting your female friends help you heal your life, you were discovering some of what men *can't* do for you. Perhaps my comments about the opposite sex were a rude awakening. Men are strange beasts to us women. And, if you're anything like me, you probably began wondering: *If women heal women, what is the point of men?* Aside from providing sperm to create children, and perhaps offering financial support, what do we need them for? My assistant says, "Lawn care and house maintenance!" But is that all there is? And how are we to understand them? (Parenthetically, the lessons of this chapter about men don't apply to sociopaths.)

Strange as this may seem, we women need men to bring forth our sensual, sexual, and nurturing natures. Their presence in our lives is necessary for us to be able to see and be our full selves! We need their bravado, desire to take care of us (in the ways that men do), passion, and adoration; we need their fix-it mentality, urge to win and conquer, impatience with emotionality, and take-charge attitudes . . . along with their need for *us!* We rely on men to bring forth the best of our feminine natures, to reassure and cherish us and to make us laugh! They can be *so* funny . . . just by being who they are!

"Men!" we'll say to a female friend or even a woman we don't know who happens to be standing behind us in the supermarket checkout line. And we'll exchange knowing looks or perhaps even belly laughs. We women understand what that "Men!" means. They are *so* silly.

We all know about men and asking for directions. They won't do it, no matter how lost they are. And when we suggest they stop the car for input, they'll say some of the funniest things. Like when my man and I were looking for the hotel where we had a reservation. He drove through the whole town, passing by at least 30 open shops. By the time we were leaving the city limits, it was clear to me that we must have passed our turnoff. And, of course, he wanted to keep going! When I suggested we stop and ask for guidance, he told me there was no one to ask! The 30 shopkeepers didn't register for him! There wasn't a gas station.

As I'm writing this chapter, my man has been away for all of two days of a weeklong business trip. And I miss his hugs, smiles, input, and kookiness. I'm happier *with* him than when we're apart. I laugh and sing more! In fact, he often says he feels like he's living in a musical! And it's easier for me to keep the small stuff in perspective when he's around.

Men balance out our intensity. Their fix-it-and-move-on approach can help keep us from getting mired in upheaval and distress. Their hugs, "I love you" statements, and commitment to stand by us (even when they haven't got a clue about why we're so upset) can help us weather some stormy emotional seas. And their eagerness to take on all sorts of chores, make a meal and clean up afterward, take us out on the town, and bring us flowers can light up our lives. And love, not money, is really what makes the world go 'round! We're altered for good by loving and being loved in return.

But men are quite different from women. And in order for us to have satisfying and workable relationships with them, we need to understand those differences. We can't expect them to be like us. If we do, we'll keep going to the dry well for water—and we'll probably die of thirst.

What You Should Know about Men

So what do you need to know about men if you're to have successful involvements with them? What are the key points? Well, I'm going to go through a few of them with you, but you'd probably do well to read some other books on the topic. A popular title is the planetary *Men Are from Mars, Women Are from Venus,* by John Gray, Ph.D. Another good one is *7 Things He'll Never Tell You . . . But You Need to Know,* by Dr. Kevin Leman. There are others, and I suggest you read whichever titles speak to you.

But what are some of the important facts about men? What do they most need? How do they think? And what really matters to them?

Well, men really are just boys grown tall. And, yes, in many ways the only difference between men and boys is the price of their toys! Little girls, and women, are relational. We talk a lot! Little boys, and men, are competitive. They're driven by their desire to win, conquer, and be the best. Their conquests are what they talk about. And they rarely, if ever, share their fears, imperfections, or limitations with one another. They don't even reveal what we would consider the crucial details of their lives with their closest friends, while women routinely learn intimate facts about the lives of other women they meet at their nail or hair-salon appointments!

Remember—women are relational, while guys are action figures. And men are always trying to be superheroes!

Guys need us to respect them and their accomplishments. No matter how successful they are in society's terms, they desperately want to be heroes in *our* eyes. They thrill to be our Prince Charmings, knights in shining armor, saviors, rescuers, and champions. They desperately want us to let them be winners. And it's crucial that we allow them to do things for us in their own ways, even if we think *we* could do some of them better! They need us to value them in this way.

We women are different. We want to be loved and cherished. We feel valued when we're connected in that way. We rarely need to conquer, win, be right, or be heroines. We desire affection, while men yearn for respect. We're totally different, but it's easy for us to honor the differences between the sexes if we understand and recognize them for what they are.

Men's brains are different from women's. We process multiple things at the same time. Our brains have many more interrelated areas acting at once. By contrast, men's brains aren't so busy. Fewer areas are active at any given moment in time. Men don't experience all the connections that we women make in a heartbeat. They can't! So, it's absurd for us to expect them to. They have, in a sense, more of a one-track mind.

And that leads us into another significant gender difference. While women are into romance and love, guys have sex on their minds almost all the time. A typical man will have about 50 to 60 sexual thoughts a day. Some of these will be quick, passing flashes; while others will be thoughts that last several minutes. An exposed arm, a woman in tight jeans, an attractive TV newscaster, or a sexual joke from a colleague may trigger the thought-form. The man may wonder what "she" looks like naked, what her breasts feel like, or what it would be like to have intercourse with her from behind! And, within a few moments, that sexual idea will vanish . . . and he'll be right back to focusing on the work project on this desk. Until another sexual thought emerges . . . and so on!

Men are highly sexual beings, and they feel the need for regular release and expression of their sexuality. They do best if they're loved and welcomed in physical embrace by the women in their lives. And if they're satisfied in their sexual lives, they're usually happy, faithful, and anxious to please and pleasure their partners. They really want to be good (actually, *great*) lovers. And they need us to tell them what works for us and how fabulous they are. We make their days when we desire and enjoy our lovemaking sessions with them. And the strength they derive from a satisfying sexual life can go a long way toward mitigating the negative impact of the other challenges and stresses they face every day. If you feed and compliment your man in this way, he'll slay dragons (or the cockroaches on your bathroom floor) for you! Very little of what you want from him will seem like too much . . . as long as you know how to ask him for things!

It's All about Communication

Which brings us into the realm of communication between the sexes. Men and women process things differently. Women need to talk and listen a lot. Men need the CliffsNotes version. They just want to hear the problem, request, or solution. They hate being asked the "Why?" question . . . because they don't usually *know* why they do things.

The more we ask them why, the more they'll tell us that we're analyzing too much. "Why can't you just accept it—or love me the way I am?" they'll say. Men view our attempts to understand them as a lack of acceptance or respect for who and how they are! Unless we women realize this fact, we'll feel pushed away, shut out, and shut up by our men.

And, of course, when we react from our hurt places, they won't understand why we're so sensitive! We'll feel more hurt. They'll get more frustrated and critical. And the whole thing will spiral quickly out of control. "You just don't understand me . . . I don't feel heard" and so on will characterize our ongoing interactions. *We'll* feel unloved, attacked, and pushed away. *They'll* feel criticized and disrespected.

So, how are we to communicate with men? Well, we need to banish the "Why?" question from our lexicon. We must realize that men are very vulnerable to perceived rejection and, like the little boys grown tall that they are, are easily wounded. While women have many friends whom we open ourselves up to, they have almost none. In all likelihood, *you're* the only one your man opens himself up to. So, when you criticize him, he'll take it *really* hard. And he'll experience some of your questions and desires to understand him as attacks . . . even when you haven't made any judgment whatsoever!

Being the way we are as women, we experience guys as hurtful, insensitive, and even cold when they have no awareness of coming across to us that way. They say they're "just kidding," tell us what they think is "nothing personal," and so on. And, unfortunately, they tend to feel like total failures if they get wind of the fact that they've hurt us. They hate to see us cry. They don't have any idea why we're upset. The whole scene makes them feel inadequate. They can't "fix it"—or, in other words, they can't make the hurt go away!

Not only that . . . when men feel scared, confused, or inadequate, they tend to get overwhelmed or emotionally flooded. They can feel *so* much that they don't know *what* they're feeling. They're not like us. Emotional intensity scrambles their brains on a *regular* basis. They can't think straight. Remember that they have one-track minds. Their cognitive functions get easily clouded, and they say and do stupid things to create space. The more we press them to stay and communicate with us when they're in a flooded state, the more they'll hurt us and push us away.

So, don't ask for trouble. Give your man a lot of space when he's irritable in that way. Pack him a lunch and send him out the door . . . or call a friend; go out for coffee, alone; or if nothing else, go into another room and calm yourself down. If he tells you he needs space, welcome it. Wish him a good time away from you, and use the distance from him to care for yourself.

You can only approach him once he has calmed down and you've gotten back in touch with your own radiance, power, and balance. So, welcome the opportunity to let your women friends help you get there. And then, in your own mind, try to put yourself into his shoes. What might have triggered his intense response? What did you say, do, or miss?

Why am I urging you to think this way? Because you've got to do a lot of the processing for both of you. Remember that your brain is more adept at this than his is. So, see what you can figure out. Once you do that, you'll know how to communicate with him when you two reconvene.

I think an example would be helpful at this point. This one comes from my call-in radio show on **HayHouseRadio.com**:

> Debbie called in from North Dakota with a question about communication issues in her marriage. She'd been married for 20 years and had suffered from a bout of clinical depression several years before. At

that time, her husband got involved with someone else for a while. The affair was over, and the couple had worked through it. But Debbie still didn't know "how to communicate with him." She was using all the communication tools I've already taught you in Chapter 9. Yet, she wasn't getting anywhere. He would put up walls and refuse to talk to her.

I asked her to give me an example of the problem. She described a scene: He had a stressful day at work. The kids were really excited about going trick-or-treating. And they were somewhat pushy with him about going out when he got home from work that day. He snapped and yelled at them. Then, when Debbie tried to tell him that his reaction scared her, he got more angry and withdrawn. The situation went from bad to worse.

"You can't use those tools with men when they're overwhelmed with emotion," I told her. "Their brains are different. They can't process what you're telling them. They're flooded with emotion, and they don't even know why they're snapping at their kids. They absolutely can't handle hearing how *you* are feeling in response. Your words just make them more overwhelmed and angry."

Debbie got it immediately. It made sense. That's exactly what had happened. And she'd seen the dynamic play out for more than 20 years. "What am I supposed to do, then?" she asked. "Can I talk to him about it later?"

I responded, "Yes, you can, but there's a particular way to do it. And this isn't easy. You have to calm yourself down first. Then you must talk to him alone and approach him when you're ready to be loving and supportive. At that point, you can ask him to tell you about his hard day at work. As the conversation goes on, you'll be able to let him know that his reaction to the kids tipped you off about how stressed he must have been, because he doesn't usually respond to them like that. Eventually, you might even choose to tell him that he scares you when he reacts in anger. If he's calm enough, he'll be able to hear you and own his part. He may even apologize."

Debbie thanked me for the guidance. She was helped by my words. They rang true for her. And she hung up having acquired a new, necessary communication skill. I found myself wishing that someone had taught it to me years before I learned it by trial and error!

So, what's the take-home point for you in this illustration? Effectively communicating with your guy (or with any guy for that matter) requires you to build a lot of the bridges. When he's strung out, you'll need to let your female friendships heal you so that you can step into his world from your place of wisdom and radiance. You're much more capable of holding myriad emotions and sorting out what's going on. And if you draw on your womanly gifts, you'll enable your man to give you all of what your heart desires from him . . . and probably a little bit more! He needs you to help him . . . but to do so, you have to treat him like a wounded little boy. You can't ask anything from him. You must love and support him. If you're able to do that, he'll feel understood and validated. Then he'll pay you back tenfold!

Grasshopper Minds

Let's move on to another aspect of the way men think and what this next difference means for us. Most men have what I lovingly like to call *grasshopper minds*. They don't process things in the linear, focused, and interconnected way most women do. They jump around from one thought to another. And in their communication with us, they often leave out the typical connections and transitions that we invariably make when we speak.

So, we women often wonder where *that* idea came from when they start telling us something about a co-worker while we're in the midst of another conversation with them. We immediately recognize the implications they hadn't thought of when they tell us that they'll be away on business the following Monday through Thursday. We'll know they were going to coach a soccer game on Monday, take their secretaries out for Administrative Professionals Day on Wednesday, and host their buddies for a card game on Thursday evening. We're prone to being hurt when they forget to ask us about our doctor's appointments, to request the agreed-upon time off from work so we can go on vacation together, or to pick up the bottle of wine they committed to bringing home for that evening's dinner guests.

Men's brains jump around the same way Mexican jumping beans bounce around in your hands. Ideas pop up here, go down over there, and reemerge at some later time when you least expect them to. Women's brains, unless we have attention deficit disorder, don't work like that. And their style rattles us!

Given our gender differences, it's really easy for the sexes to run amok in communication. We women are apt to misinterpret men's "jumpiness." We tend to assume a lack of interest or concern. We do that because that's what it would mean if *we* behaved as they do! But they're different! So, beware of assuming. In fact, I suggest you make a totally different type of assumption: *Assume* you have no idea why he's done what he did. Give him the benefit of doubt. And gently, without sounding judgmental, ask him if there's a connection you missed, for instance, or if he's aware of the scheduling conflict you've already recognized. You'll be amazed by how much he'll appreciate your assistance . . . but he probably won't tell you he does directly! It will show up in another way!

Men, Women, and Emotion

Now, let's look at one additional crucial difference between the sexes. It concerns something else about the way men process emotions. Most men are in touch with two feeling states (1) happy or okay, and (2) angry. They don't connect with the range of emotional experiences we have. And, beyond that, they have a very limited repertoire when they're upset. They tend to get quiet or withdrawn, pouty, passive-aggressive, or angry in a fairly immature temper-tantrum kind of way. They're not particularly talented at giving voice to their feelings or needs. And they can completely change the energy in a room with their demeanor and actions.

Men are rarely aware of their power in this regard, and they're often out of touch with the fact that they're even bothered!

So, how are we to handle them? Well, we can try to get behind the distress with loving-kindness. We can treat them like wounded children. We can retreat into our own space when they get testy. And we can ask them to do their best to identify and communicate *their* need for space in a caring way. Finally, we can be tolerant and respectful of their ways of being. Remember that when they calm down, they can be awesome and magical!

Don't allow yourself to be put out by the differences between men and women. Yes, men can be exasperating, but so can we be—to them! And we each desperately need the other to give us the joy, fulfillment, pleasure, and passion that only male-female intimacy allows. In the next chapter, you'll be learning the importance of inviting joy, passion, and pleasure into your life.

Chapter 12

INVITE JOY, PLEASURE, AND PASSION INTO YOUR LIFE

*R*omance and steamy sex sells movies, books, and magazines. And these forms of media rarely sell well *without* it! There's a reason for that pattern, and it underlies the lesson of this chapter: *you need to invite joy, pleasure, and passion into your life!*

Romance, passion, and sexual pleasure are among the most basic drives and healers on our planet. We humans need the nitrous-oxide boost, endorphin high, and whole-body healing potential brought about by a vibrant sex life. Our sleep, level of energy and joy, and resistance to strokes and hypertension are affected by the quality of our sex lives. Loving, nurturing touch affects immune function and saves lives. Babies who aren't held and cuddled fail to thrive . . . and eventually die.

A good love life helps us to *love life* more fully. It can kick-start our days, lift our spirits, and provide us a safe harbor to rest in. It buffers and buttresses us. And it can bless us with perspective, balance, and inner peace.

Our bodies long to be touched, caressed, fondled, aroused, and fulfilled; and when they're cared for in these ways, we feel better. We're more hopeful, self-loving, empowered, and renewed. Remember that '60s bumper sticker "Make Love Not War"? Loving behavior heals us . . . and the whole world, too!

Your Inner Goddess

So what does all this sex talk have to do with healing your life when your world explodes? What exactly are you supposed to pursue, and how are you to do it? Should you start having random sex with every interested party? Or go to bars and begin picking up guys? Or *insist* on regular sex play from your current partner? Heck no! But you need to begin inviting pleasure into your life. And that may well start with pursuing a new passion or long-standing dream, or with learning your own anatomy well enough to enable you to love and pleasure yourself!

You see, it's likely that you got to this point in your life because you weren't caring for your inner goddess very well. *I* surely wasn't! And you probably carry around a lot of negative ideas and beliefs about yourself, your sexuality, and what you deserve. Most women do. It's also likely that you doubt yourself and dislike your body—feeling too fat, unattractive, or "old." And chances are extremely good that you were taught to focus on love, romance, and caretaking to the exclusion of self-realization and satisfying sexual relationships.

Over and over again I've been struck by the fact that we women haven't been taught the importance of attraction, physical "fit," and great sex to the pleasure and viability of our long-term romantic partnerships. But chemistry, sexual attraction, and a powerful desire to be intimate with the men we date is necessary to building fulfilling and passionate relationships with them! Let go of that double standard that women who crave sex are tramps, while guys who flirt and fool around a lot are studs! The clichés say that men and women are *totally* different. Men just want sex, and women only desire romance and love. Period. End of story. That's just "the way it is." But nothing could be further from the truth.

Women are sexual beings, and we have just as much fun in bed, or on the kitchen floor, as men do.

I can't even tell you how many times I've sat with women in my clinical office and listened to them lament the lack of sexual intimacy in their marriages. Often they've wanted what their partners couldn't or wouldn't provide, or they've pined for a partner whom they found exciting and attractive . . . letting on that they've *never* really experienced their current mates in that way! They've settled for the good provider, the nice guy, or a man who was "husband material." Or they just hadn't realized how important sexual attraction really was or how significant it would become for them. They've deferred their dreams and desires. And they're just beginning to wake up!

So, here's the deal. Healing your life when your world explodes will be much easier for you if you unleash your inner goddess instead of keeping her under wraps. Even if you don't realize it now, she's actually longing to get out and have fun! And the more you help her assume her rightful place in your life, the more joyful and fulfilled you'll be.

I've worked with many women whose sexual impulses got so buried by dull marriages that they stopped realizing that they had any interest in sex at all! One of the most transformative books for them (and for me, I must add) has been Gail Sheehy's *Sex and the Seasoned Woman: Pursuing the Passionate Life*. It's about a whole universe of lusty women who are redefining what middle age is about. They're discovering a new identity, intimacy, and passion in life . . . and their sexual relationships are more fulfilling than they've ever been. And there are *millions* of women like this! I'm one . . . and you can be, too! So, let's begin to look at how you can get there!

Oh God, you may be thinking. *This book has gone from self-help to X-rated. Get me out. I'm not ready for this.* Or you may be breathing a deep sigh of relief . . . because you've been dancing around this issue in your own mind for years and have felt too embarrassed to let on. Or you may have realized your need to reclaim your passionate side, but felt hopeless about the possibility of sexual joy or clueless about how to achieve it. Or you could be one of those rare fully realized, sensual women who can skip over this chapter! If you meet the criteria of the totally evolved sex goddess, I'd love to meet you! I'm sure you can teach us all some great lessons. (Although I doubt you exist . . . since every women I've ever met has struggled some in this realm.)

So how are you to start connecting with your sensual, sexual side? And is the only path to pleasure via dating and romance? You may be too burned or scared by your betrayal experience to start with that. So how are you to begin? What should you do?

Well, as you've already learned, you can only bring to yourself what you're ready to receive. And what you focus on, you create. Remember, your intentions create your experiences.

So, I want you to start focusing on your beauty and sensuality. Begin allowing yourself to desire sexual satisfaction. Know that you're a sexual being who deserves joy, pleasure, and fulfillment. And affirm yourself and your body every day. Look in the mirror and say, "You are beautiful." Or smile at your image as you wash your face each morning and say, "Good morning, gorgeous!" Study your naked body—your profile, breasts, arms, legs, and neck. Then talk to each and every part of your body in a loving way. You are aged to perfection!

Begin touching and fondling yourself in various areas and in different ways. Learn what turns you on, what pleasures you, and how you like to be caressed. Buy—and wear—beautiful and sexy lingerie. Experiment with oils and sex toys. Read romance novels and erotic literature for women. Fantasize, dream, listen to sensual music . . . do whatever helps you to connect with your inner goddess. Some great books to aid you in this self-discovery process are *The Secret Pleasures of Menopause* (which is not *just* about menopause), by Christiane Northrup, M.D.; *The Age of Miracles,* by Marianne Williamson; and *Secrets & Mysteries: The Glory and Pleasure of Being a Woman,* by Denise Linn. I've read and learned some valuable tips from each of them! I'm sure you will, too!

Okay . . . so, what about dating, building romance and intimacy with men, and making yourself vulnerable again? That's a big part of this chapter's lesson. Are you worried, insecure, or excited about moving into that stage? For most women who've been burned, the answer is: *all of the above.* No matter what your response, you're not alone. We've all been there. Moving on is scary *and* empowering, but what exactly are you to do?

Well, in order to be successful in this realm, you must engage fully in the process. You've got to put your whole self into the thing like that "Hokey Pokey" song suggests. You can't realize what you're not ready to accept. You'll be working at creating your heart's desire, so you'll need to use the tools you learned in Chapter 7.

The Importance of Ritual or Ceremony

For many women who've been burned, another step is necessary. It involves using ritual or ceremony to symbolically *end* that which needs to be finished emotionally and *welcome* that which is meant to come next. Some examples include burning your wedding dress, participating in a *get* or Jewish ritual-divorce service, and calling together your women friends to toast your newfound freedom at a divorce party. If you're staying in a relationship, maybe you need to have a commitment ceremony or renew your vows. Be inventive and create your own "let go of the past and move on to the future" ritual. Draw on friends, spiritual traditions, and other cultures for ideas. Be fluid with this.

As I was writing this chapter, my fabulous assistant, Teresa, shared her story with me. It was a great example of the lesson you just read about, so I asked her to write it down for you. Here it is . . .

> *Dating has always been tricky for me. It's not finding dates that's the problem, but rather finding someone with whom I feel that special connection. I've been involved for years in a running group that has a large membership, and I've met some good guys there. I've also tried, on and off, online dating services and have had luck meeting some very nice guys.*
>
> *The problem was that while there was nothing really wrong with the guys I was meeting, I wasn't feeling that special "zing" with any of them. I wanted that crazy-in-love feeling. Eventually, I started to think that maybe it just didn't happen when you got older. Maybe it was just something that younger people felt. Perhaps a love relationship was just about companionship, friendship, and common interests. I don't think those are bad traits to share with someone, but I wanted more than that.*
>
> *At the same time, I'd been reading and studying a lot about creating the life you want. I'd been using the tools and techniques I'd learned to set up the rest of my life the way I wanted it to be. And I was doing really well. I was choosing how my life would be, rather than letting myself be buffeted around by random events. So it occurred to*

me that perhaps I should be utilizing the same techniques in my love life. I was ready to take charge and have the relationship that I was searching for.

I gave some thought to the whole process and decided I would start out by making a very detailed list of my perfect man. I used words and small drawings to describe everything about him. I included looks, personality traits, likes and dislikes, goals, job, and (this is a big one) how he would feel about me. I included every single small detail I could possibly think of. The list took me about a week to complete. I would add a couple of words or drawings, set the list aside, and come back to it when I thought of something else to add. Some of the items were so nitpicky that I felt a little foolish adding them. But then I would remind myself that this was my list. I was describing my perfect man.

When I decided that I was finally finished with my description, I took the list and cut out all the little words and drawings. I took my pile of little pieces of paper outside and lit them on fire in a small metal pan. As I watched the smoke curl up toward the sky, I imagined that it would ride on the wind currents and find that man I had described. I silently asked the universe to bring him to me.

I thought I would give the universe a little help. I rejoined the online dating service I'd used in the past. Then I got contacted by Chris. I didn't think we were much of a match when I first saw his profile. He'd just moved to town and was only looking for someone to go to the occasional dinner, movie, or baseball game with. I responded to him because I thought it would be nice to have a new friend. By the third date, we were hopelessly in

love with each other and dating seriously. I've been seeing
him for a year now. He is exactly the guy I described in
my list! A perfect match.

I'm grateful to have my assistant, Teresa! The universe brought her to me at just the right time in my life. The world really works that way sometimes! Teresa actually began to work for me just weeks before my world exploded. She'd answered my ad for a personal assistant because she wanted a varied job with lots of new challenges and duties. And my professional life as a doctor, columnist, radio-show host, and author fit that bill. Little did either of us realize *how* interesting and varied her job would end up being! We both joke about it today.

She's been my friend, confidante, "wife," coparent, paralegal, and sounding board. In addition to being the personal assistant that I was originally looking for, Teresa has been a godsend to me. And now she's even helping *you* by contributing her own experiences and wisdom to this chapter's lesson. And she's got a lot to teach. Pay attention to the changes she made and the ceremony she created to welcome her heart's desire. She brainstormed and followed her intuition. *You* can do the same thing.

Think about it. What sort of ceremony, ritual, or rite-of-passage celebration appeals to you? What might you choose to write, burn, share, toast, welcome, or give away? Do you need to pen a letter and bury it, feng-shui your home, or visit a medicine man? Do you think it might help to buy yourself a piece of jewelry to replace the one on your finger you've chosen (or needed) to take off? Might you benefit from ripping up and recycling those old love letters that feel love*less* now? Just what might you do to symbolically end that which needs to be finished emotionally and welcome that which is meant to come next? I urge you to do what both helps you emotionally close those chapters of your life that are finished and enables you to step fully into the next ones. Your new story is about to begin!

Dating and Romance

Here she goes, you may be thinking. *We're in the sex-and-passion chapter; and now she's going to tell me to go out, date, and have sex. But I'm not ready to do that. I've gotta shape up, redo myself, get a makeover, lose 10 to 20 pounds, and have plastic surgery first. No one I desire is going to find me attractive like* <u>this!</u>

"Wrong! Wrong! Wrong!" I tell you. Stop worrying and get moving. You need to love and be loved. It's good for you.

Anyway, you're fabulous just the way you are! And almost every guy will tell you that confident, sexy women are way more interesting and sexually arousing to them than gorgeous women who are uncomfortable in their bodies. Sexy women are self-assured, self-accepting, sensual, and at ease flirting with men and inviting male attention. They're joyful, and happy to share their joy. Sensual women are fun in bed and anxious to please their partners, and they let men know how to pleasure *them*. And, believe it or not, nothing turns most men on more than successfully pleasuring their women!

So, is dating and building relationships all about sex, and is that the kind of passion you need to cultivate to heal your life? Well . . . no . . . not exactly, but sex, passion, and romance are pretty fundamental for most of us. And remember— love does make the world go 'round.

But do all of us experience love in the same way? Is sex or physical touch, for example, equally important to men and women—or, for that matter, to *all* men or *all* women? Well, the answer to that question is *no!* Different people feel and express love in different ways. And we each have a tendency to assume that our mates, dates, and loved ones are just like us. Often we're wrong.

Gary Chapman has written a best-selling book about this issue called *The Five Love Languages: How to Express Heartfelt Commitment to Your Mate.* In it, he identifies five specific love languages, or ways different people express love. These are *quality time, words of affirmation, gifts, acts of service,* and *physical touch.* And, he says, we each have a primary love language. He describes each language in a separate chapter and teaches us how to identify our own primary one and those of our partners. He then shows us how to ask for and express love in language suited to the receiver. He says that in most relationships, each partner has a different primary love language.

You probably know what I'm going to say next. It's crucial that you learn what you *and your partner* need to feel loved if your relationship is to endure, thrive, and bring you both joy. I urge you to read Chapman's book. Incorporate his teachings in building the love life your heart desires. And remember to bring your inner goddess to the table!

Dating Tips

Okay. It's time to deal with dating! I'd like to give you some specific tips and suggestions to help you navigate the dating scene. Perhaps you're entering it after having been "out of the loop" for a long time. Or maybe you've been in it for a while but are getting nowhere fast! Alternatively, maybe you're contemplating whether and how to date in the latter half of this century. Whatever your story, you'll likely learn something from the following list. Use what appeals to you!

1. Be open, friendly, and outgoing. You'll invite people to you if you're friendly, accepting, and welcoming. They'll want to get to know you and to share themselves with you. So say hello to strangers, offer to share a table with a man who is alone in a coffee shop, or strike up a conversation with the guy behind you in the supermarket line.

2. Approach men; don't wait to *be* approached. Guys like women who reach out to them. It's hard to be the one who approaches the opposite sex all the time. Remember that guys fear rejection, and some of them are really shy. Most men appreciate a gentle expression of interest in them, so give it a whirl. You'll never know where it might take you if you don't!

3. Be realistic—don't settle for crumbs, but don't be too picky, either. No man (or woman) is perfect. Remember that we're all human. So I urge you to believe in your heart's desire . . . but to realize that your ideal man may come to you in disguise. He may not at first look at all like you expect him to, but don't be fooled: There's a reason we all like those stories about frogs turning into princes upon being kissed! The imperfect guy may turn out to be a perfect fit! And if not, he'll teach you something you need to know.

4. Look at every date as an opportunity to learn something. Whenever you meet, greet, or break bread with a man, you have opportunity to *grow yourself!* Pay attention to what you like in him . . . and what you don't. Notice what makes you laugh, what he does to interest you, and how he shuts you down. Do you enjoy yourself in his company? Is he funny, caring, intellectual, fascinating, or boring? Do you want to touch him? Would you enjoy spending more time with him? Do the minutes or hours fly by, or are you counting the seconds until you can respectfully get up and thank him for the cup of coffee? Each date has the potential to teach you something. Allow yourself to learn its lesson.

5. Be patient. Don't rush things. Beware of investing too much energy in trying to make it work between you and any man. Don't push commitment. Be patient. If it's good enough now, stay with it. If it's meant to work out over the long haul, it will of its own accord. Don't hold on too tight. You squeeze the life out of the most vibrant of connections when you do. Enjoy what is pleasurable, for as long as it serves you both well!

6. Cultivate acceptance—don't try to change him. The only person you can change is yourself. Listen carefully to what each man tells you about who he is and what matters to him. You must accept him just as he is. If you like who he is enough, continue to see him. If you don't, check out right now! He may never change one iota. Don't make the mistake of staying with someone *because* of his potential. It's a losing battle.

7. Be careful not to confuse sex with love. Guys who are into you will want to do it with you . . . even if they aren't wild enough about you to want to wake up to you the next morning too many days in a row. If you want to have sex with a guy whom you haven't yet qualified for the longer haul, do it! Just be really clear about *what* you're doing. And read the next tip first. (And please, use a condom!) Don't expect love to follow sex for an noninvested guy!

8. Consider using my assistant's six-date rule. If you're looking for more than a sexual relationship with a guy, don't have sex with him before you've gone on six dates. If he's into more of you than your body, and you're still into him, he'll be there by date number six. Then you can have a fun time exploring each other's anatomy! This "rule" can keep you from getting hurt by making yourself more vulnerable than you might want to be if the guy is just looking for sex!

9. Love the one you're with. Avoid thinking the grass is always greener on the other side of the fence. If you can't enjoy the company of the man you're dating, stop wasting your time and his. Nothing good can come of staying for either of you. If you're not into him, it's not good for him to have you stick around!

10. Chemistry is crucial. Don't allow yourself to underestimate the importance of physical attraction. Remember that desire is born of attraction. And a satisfying sex life heals you. A nonexistent or passionless one is miserable. Don't commit to or do it with guys who don't *really* turn you on.

11. If he "dumps" you, it's a gift! Just like in the lessons you learned from your betrayal experience, if he's not into you enough to want to be with you, you're *way better off* without him. You need and deserve to be valued and cherished. Dust yourself off, thank the universe for giving you the push to move on, and get going, girl!

12. Take good care of yourself and stay out of harm's way. Whether you realize it or not, not everyone is who they say they are or has the history they give you. You've heard, read, and maybe even lived horror stories already. I urge you to check out the men you choose to date. You can learn about their marital status, possible criminal background, and property-tax history though online searches of public records. You can even Google the person's name and sometimes find out if the story he has told you is consistent with other information. Don't be shy about doing this. Your health and safety may depend on it! Make sure you meet in a public place the first few times. Don't tell your address to men you don't yet know. Don't invite them into your home or go into theirs. If they push you on this, get out, quick! They're trouble. Good guys will accept your need to be careful and cautious!

13. When you're ready, true love will appear. And you won't have to work too hard to make it happen. As long as you're doing your part to create your heart's desire, it will come to you. And if it hasn't come after a lot of searching, you're setting up a wall! If you think you might be, please pick up and read *Don't Get Lucky, Get Smart: Why Your Love Life Sucks and What You Can Do About It,* by Alan Cohen. It's a great book!

14. Trust your gut. If you feel weird about a guy, get out! If you're drawn to him, go with it! Don't be foolish, but don't overanalyze, either. The heart knows things the brain can take a long time to realize! Trust your inner wisdom!

15. Know, affirm, and believe that you'll succeed! You will find your heart's desire. You're capable, beautiful, awesome, fabulous, and deserving. And you *will* experience great passion and pleasure. It's yours for the asking!

In Closing

In closing, I want to remind you to invite joy, pleasure, and passion into your life. Your inner goddess is aching to come out! Let yourself care for her! Remember that healing your life when your world explodes will go much better if you love yourself and let others love you, too!

Use the tips, tools, and strategies you've learned in this chapter—and any others you find helpful—to build a fulfilling and passionate sex life! You deserve the joy and healing power it will bring you! And what's more . . . it's about time you started having a little *fun!* In the next chapter, you'll learn how to stay present to the moment, so whenever you're ready for that lesson, turn the page!

Chapter 13

STAY PRESENT TO THE GIFT OF THE MOMENT

In the last chapter, you learned to invite joy, passion, and pleasure into your life. You focused on releasing your inner goddess and letting yourself have fun. I hope you're enjoying what she brings into your life, but I imagine that you still struggle with worry at times and get off track. In this chapter, I want to teach you how to stay present to the gift of the here-and-now.

It's hard to stay in the moment. In fact, most of us are stressed-out almost all of the time! We walk around feeling irritable, overwhelmed, jumpy, scared, exhausted, and strung out. We're not on top of our game. We're worried about our finances, health, relationships, kids, planet, and futures. And those of us who have been betrayed often worry more than those who haven't been!

We all buy more and more stuff to fill us up, and spend billions of dollars on medications to help us calm down and fall asleep. We numb ourselves with alcohol, online distractions, TV, and movies. We future-forecast, revisit past traumas, and try to analyze the ineffable. We just won't quit. We seem to be addicted to worry and distraction.

Yet each time we get caught up in these negative thought patterns and avoidance strategies, we rob ourselves of the joy that is available to us right now. In our heart of hearts, we know that the only thing we really have is the current moment. Nothing is guaranteed. And no matter what we think, do, or focus on, we can't change the past or control the future. Even so, we constantly worry about yesterday and tomorrow, and we keep ourselves stuck in ruts whenever we do so!

Don't Sweat the Small Stuff . . .

In order to heal your life after betrayal, you have to stop worrying so much. You can't possibly bring joy into your future life if the pleasures of today elude you.

You must begin to welcome and value every moment as you live it. Think about this! Even though you're worried about your future, you're okay right now. So ask yourself: *What is working well for me today? What is bringing me joy? What am I grateful for in this moment?* Remember—*you draw to yourself what you focus on.* Do you want it to be peace or worry? Joy or sadness? Hope or fear?

I'd like you to consider the following question:

> *Is it possible that the little things you worry about all the time aren't nearly as important as you think they are?*

You probably have an immediate "yes" response. Almost all of us relate to this dynamic. The universality of this problem is the main reason that the book *Don't Sweat the Small Stuff . . . and It's All Small Stuff* is such a success. We all "sweat" stuff a lot and think our worries matter. But we also know deep down inside that we're often spinning our wheels, wasting energy, and focusing on insignificant issues.

In my book *10 Steps to Take Charge of Your Emotional Life,* I tell the following story:

When I was about 18 years old, I escorted groups of adults two, three, and four times my age to Eastern Europe and what was then the Soviet Union. I worked for a U.S.-based tour-packaging company, and my job was to travel with the groups and make sure that everything ran smoothly. I worked with the local city guides, hotels, airlines, and so on. For some reason, I found very little of it overwhelming, but I did always worry: *What if we get to Moscow or Leningrad and the local guide with the bus doesn't meet me at the airport? This could be a big problem.*

In the USSR at that time, the government owned and ran all tourist operations—including the hotels and local tour-guide agencies. For reasons of "security," visiting groups weren't told where they'd be staying in advance. The Intourist (the official state travel agency) guide who met us at the airport would tell us what hotel we'd be going to and have a bus ready to take us there. I kept thinking, *How will I possibly know where to go and what to do with my group of 30 to 40 tourists if no local help appears?* I would worry . . . a lot!

And then, guess what? It happened! I got to Moscow with 35 travelers, and no guide appeared. In the moment, I had no time to worry; I had to *act*. So I designated one group member as the leader, parked all my tourists around him, and told him to keep everyone together until I returned. I'd find out what to do. And off I went. I quickly located an Intourist representative in the airport who got on the phone immediately. In rapid-fire Russian, he sorted out what had happened, secured a bus for us, ascertained where we were meant to stay, and told me that our guide would be at the hotel by the time we got there.

In no time flat, my group was en route to our accommodations—and no one besides me and the driver had any idea that there had even been the slightest glitch in the plans. As

I sat at the front of the bus, microphone in hand, pointing out and describing the sights along the way, I realized that my long-standing worry had been much ado about nothing. . . . So many of our worries *are!*

Today, whenever I hear myself or any of my patients say, "What will I do if . . . ?" and then go on to describe some worry about *what might be,* I reply, "We'll deal with it when we get there." Reminding myself and those I serve that there will be a solution when the time comes is deeply comforting. This strategy allows us all to relax and let go of worry. I suggest you use it.

I personally have returned to this lesson over and over again in dealing with my betrayal and its aftermath. Doing so has kept me sane! When, for instance, I had to write massive checks for legal fees month after month, I found myself getting really fearful. I worried that I'd run out of money and be unable to provide for myself and my kids. So I found a way to calm myself down: Each time I made out a huge check, I also wrote an affirming statement in my checkbook next to my record of the payment. It would be something like: "Don't worry! It's going to work out." These reminders helped me settle into the moment. Eventually, everything *did* work out for me. I'm not, of course, destitute. I'm actually doing well. My worry was much ado about nothing! Think about how you might implement this strategy in your own life.

Here's another way to bring your focus to the here-and-now . . . get back to basics! Your health depends on it. Consider:

- *What matters?*
- *What pleasures me today?*
- *What am I grateful for?*
- *What works, and how can I grow the good stuff?*

If you're like most people, you don't visit those basics enough! Try to change that pattern to stay in the now.

Another tool that you can use to stay in the present is to consciously revisit the lessons of your history. You've already learned that you've suffered unnecessarily as a result of letting worry, fear, horror, and pain consume your heart, mind, and soul. You've stayed in miserable situations because you were afraid of change. You've tolerated the intolerable because you didn't actually realize how untenable the situations were or that you could leave them! You've berated, criticized, and doubted yourself when you've actually done the best you could possibly have done. You now know that you're amazing. It's time to say to yourself: "Enough is enough!" Stop torturing yourself. Let it be!

Reclaim your power, joy, and inner peace. Today is a new day. This moment is your precious gift. You deserve to experience it in its full wonder! You've earned it. You're entitled to it. You deserve it! How else can you de-stress, decompress, and honor your need for inner peace? Here are some more ideas. . . .

In my *Stop Anxiety Now Kit,* I describe a series of tools that can help you. I suggest that you experiment with them. Some are self-explanatory. They include exercise and dance; prayer, chanting, and singing; and yoga, tai chi, and qigong. Some other tools I include are affirmations (which you learned how to create in Chapter 6), relaxation techniques and guided imagery, and a cognitive-behavioral intervention that I call *thought stopping.* I'd like to teach you the thought-stopping technique so that you can use it to interrupt those worry loops that arise, derail you, and keep you from being present in the *now!*

Thought Stopping

Cognitive-behavioral techniques are crucial to the effective management of anxiety, and they rely on the powerful mind-body connection. The idea is that *the thoughts that produce and maintain anxiety can be recognized and stopped.* Worry spirals up, but it can spiral down, too. Think of escalating worry like a snowball rolling down a hill, gathering momentum and gaining in size as it goes. Now imagine that snowball hitting a wall and ceasing to move—when the bright sun appears in the sky and the temperature rises, the snow melts rapidly into a puddle. Just like the snowball, worry can completely disappear under the right conditions.

When the thoughts that fuel your worry are interrupted, the anxiety itself will begin to dissipate; therefore, I'm going to teach you a technique to interrupt those thoughts. You can use it to squash the beliefs that fuel your worry.

Examples of such beliefs include:

- *I'll never be able to live without him.*
- *I'm going to die a pauper* [or *run out of money*].
- *I'm in danger—someone is going to harm me.*
- *I'm destined to fail.*
- *I'm not good enough.*
- *I'll never be able to live my heart's desire.*

Sometimes when those anxious thoughts arise, you'll be able to interrupt them with an affirmation or a gentle reminder to settle down. But at other times, your worrisome thoughts may take on a life of their own and get you into a spiraling loop. If you can calm a thought by talking back to it, do so. But if your anxious self argues back, repeating the fearful thought and even spinning it out of control, use the thought-stopping technique to return to the present!

This technique involves the following series of steps:

1. Identify the negative thought you're telling yourself (such as *I'll never be able to live without him* or *I'm not good enough*).

2. Take a single opportunity to tell yourself something that contradicts the negative thought (for example, *I have everything I need* or *I am a worthwhile person*).

3. Begin to tell yourself to "stop it" whenever you find yourself beginning the "cascade."

4. Use reminders of any sort to help you remember to turn that negative message off.

5. Rather than allowing yourself to continue focusing on the negative thought by "talking back" to it specifically, distract yourself in any way you can. Use music, a book or magazine, television, exercise, cooking, singing, chanting, praying, deep breathing, whistling, phone calls to friends, hugs, or anything else that will keep you from returning to the thought. You want to interrupt the brain rut you're in.

6. Use this technique whenever you realize that you're engaging in a spiral of negative self-talk. You may find yourself falling into a destructive thought cycle before you even recognize what's happening; over time, however, you'll begin to identify the moments when your negative thinking is getting the better of you.

7. Stay the course. As time goes on, you'll learn to interrupt yourself faster and faster and will need to use the technique less and less.

Time to Create Your Own Thought-Stopping Tool!

In order to create your own thought-stopping tool, you'll need to identify a few things. You'll also have to create some little stop signs on index cards! So make the stop signs, and then answer the following questions:

a. "What do I tell myself that makes me anxious, or what are my escalating worries?"

b. "What will I say back to my thoughts *one time only?*" Identify a statement for each thought.

c. "What distraction(s) will I use to keep myself from thinking my worrisome thought(s)?"

d. "Where will I place stop-sign reminders?" (Some options include your dashboard, bathroom mirror, calendar, computer screen, refrigerator, telephone table, and so forth.)

To help you with this exercise, read the following examples of worrisome thoughts, along with the series of possible *one-time* responses for each of them (in bold):

- *I'm going to die a pauper.* **One day at a time . . . I have what I need for today.**

- *I'm in danger—someone's going to harm me.* **I am safe and sound right now. I stay in the moment.**

- *I'm destined to fail.* ***I create my own destiny. I live my heart's desire.***

To create your own list of distractions, think about what engages you fully, no matter how stressed you are. Feel free to pick from the following list:

- Music (listening to it or playing an instrument)
- Reading (books, magazines, or the newspaper)
- Television
- Exercising
- Cooking
- Singing
- Chanting

- Praying
- Deep breathing
- Whistling
- Meditating
- Counting
- Socializing with friends
- Hugging
- Laughing

After answering the questions, place those little stop signs you've created in the locations you've identified. Then fill in the blanks as follows on the template labeled "My Thought-Stopping Plan" on the next page:

- For *a*, write in your worrisome thought(s).
- For *b*, write down your one-time responses to your worrisome thought(s).
- For *c*, write down the locations you've placed the stop signs.
- For *d*, write down the distraction(s) you're going to use.

My Thought-Stopping Plan

When I begin to tell myself _____ [a], I will say _____ [b] back to myself one time. Then I will turn the worrisome thought off by saying "Stop it." I've put the stop signs in key places to remind me to use the technique. Those places include: _____ and _____ [c]. As soon as I say "Stop it" to myself, I will make use of my distraction(s). That means that I will _____ [d].

I realize that I may get into worrisome spirals a lot at first. I will need to say "Stop it" each time. I will read my Thought-Stopping Plan out loud twice a day. My worrisome thoughts will decrease over time. I can heal. I am committed to my wellness, and I have confidence in the power of my mind to heal my body.

As I interrupt my worrisome thoughts, my anxiety will melt away. I will experience calm and inner peace. I will become present to the gift of the moment.

If you experience spiraling worries, use the *Stop Anxiety Now* tool regularly. Read your Thought-Stopping Plan out loud at least twice a day—it's best done first thing in the morning and at the end of the workday or before bed. Reading your plan often serves two functions:

1. It becomes a powerful reminder to use the thought-stopping technique.

2. It becomes a fantastic affirmation in its own right.

Read it twice daily until you're almost free from worry for three weeks. You may then decrease your reading frequency, but cut back slowly. Even when you do stop your regular reading, an occasional booster is a good idea.

Nutritional Interventions

There are some simple nutritional interventions that you can implement to settle your nervous system and help you stay present to the moment. They include decreasing or even eliminating your use of caffeine, sugar, and artificial sweeteners.

Sometimes what we eat and drink causes us to feel anxious. Caffeine, for example, is a stimulant to the brain or central nervous system. We all respond to its energizing power, but some of us are extremely sensitive to its activating effects. We get anxious, experience an increase in heart rate and blood pressure, and become sweaty and uncomfortable.

Many drinks and medications contain caffeine—including coffee, tea, Mountain Dew, Red Bull, Midol, and No-Doz—so read labels and begin to consider your use of this substance. Are you highly sensitive to its effects? Might you want to decrease your consumption or eliminate it from your diet?

If you choose to cut down on or do away with caffeine, taper your use by a small amount every few days. This approach will keep you from feeling the uncomfortable withdrawal symptoms of headaches, depression, and fatigue.

Sugar and artificial sweeteners can affect your body in some of the same ways that caffeine does! You may notice yourself getting highly anxious when you eat a lot of simple carbohydrates (like cookies, cakes, candies, and ice cream) or when you drink bunches of diet soda. Your hormonal balance is dramatically altered by your blood-sugar and insulin levels.

And sometimes the disequilibrium established by your diet can really unsettle your nervous system. So, if you notice a possible sensitivity in this area, try cutting down on (or eliminating) your intake of simple sugars and artificial sweeteners. You can taper off if you wish, but abruptly stopping these foods isn't dangerous (my assistant says, "That's what you think—try to take them away from *me* and see what happens! . . . Ha, ha, ha!"), so use your own judgment and trust your gut.

Finally, you might want to consider adding nutritional support or medication to quell your worry. Herbal interventions and antianxiety medications can do wonders for some people. To learn more about those possibilities, pick up a copy of my book *10 Steps to Take Charge of Your Emotional Life,* or talk to your health-care provider about the best options for you and your situation.

Staying Present in Relationships

We've been spending a lot of time exploring tools to quell anxiety and worry so you'll be present to the gift of the moment. But how might you apply those strategies and concepts to the challenges that arise in relationships? Let's look at that issue now.

As we enter this "staying present to the moment" lesson in relationships, I want you to keep a few key teachings you've learned from prior chapters in mind. Here are those points:

1. Even though you make plans, the universe may have different intentions for you!

2. Life will unfold and surprise you. You can't know the details of your future in advance.

3. Timing is crucial. When you're ready for a lesson, your teacher will appear. Your gut instinct will direct you to leave, stay in, or enter a situation when it's time.

4. What feels right in the moment is correct. What feels bad in the moment is wrong.

5. What you want in this exact moment is your heart's desire.

6. You can't know for sure how you'll feel or act in a situation until you're actually in it.

7. Your intuition is brilliant. Oftentimes you make bad decisions because you don't pay attention to it.

8. You can create your heart's desire . . . one moment at a time.

A Simple Illustration Is Worth a Thousand Words

I'd like to use my own story to show you how staying-in-the-moment strategies can further a relationship. This example concerns my growing intimacy with Tom, whom I've mentioned in previous chapters. I have to give you some background information first.

From the very beginning, Tom and I felt an amazing and intense attraction to one another. To our mutual surprise, we began talking about a future together very early on. We weren't really prepared to commit to all of what that meant. Yet the discussions continued to emerge, draw us in, get us charged up, and even freak us out!

Periodically, Tom would get anxious, withdraw, and cut off all contact. He feared replaying his past awful marriage experience. He also worried that I'd decide to leave him. And *I* was anxious about his withdrawal. I feared that this fabulous guy would run away and never come back!

We would go back and forth as we grew closer and then got scared. I often found myself saying: "We're getting ahead of ourselves. Let's stop making decisions about the future and see where we are 10 to 12 months from now. If we still feel this much love for one another then, it will be clear that we're meant to keep going. Easy does it." And this "staying in the now" strategy would settle us both down.

Every so often, Tom would say to me: "You can do so much better than me. You should probably date other guys to see what's out there. You're going to wake up one day and say, 'What am I doing with this guy?'"

I would find myself replying, "If by 'better' you mean something about titles and assets, you are absolutely right. But those things don't matter to me. I know how I feel about you right now. I'm crazy about you, and I don't want to date anyone else. You make me happy. And I'm comfortable staying with what feels just right for today!" Those words would help me stay in the now . . . moment after moment . . . and they helped him, too.

Today, as I sit here writing this particular example for you, Tom and I are engaged to be married! We've been together for more than a year, and we've gotten to this place of commitment by continuing to revisit the gift of the present moment . . . one day at a time. We're now even more in love than we were a few weeks ago, and I believe our feelings will continue to grow. *But I'm not getting ahead of myself!* This moment is fabulous . . . just the way it is!

By the time you read the words I've just written, I'll be married to Tom. Timing is funny in the publishing world. Manuscripts get delivered to a publisher way before actual books are printed, so I'm telling you today's headlines. Tomorrow's story has yet to unfold. We'll all learn it when we get there!

So, let's return to the lesson of this example. By using "stay in the moment" strategies, you can achieve wonders in your relationships. You'll be able to calm your worries, regain perspective, and determine what your heart desires from moment to moment. As you honor your present wisdom, you'll gain clarity. You'll know what to say, what to do, and how to bring joy into your life. I know you can be successful . . . one minute at a time!

In Closing

Here's a recap of the material in this chapter:

You can, and must, stay present to the gift of the moment. In order to heal your life after betrayal, you have to stop worrying so much. Begin to welcome and value every moment as you live it. You have a lot of tools to help you do so. Consider whether the things you worry about all the time are much ado about nothing. Revisit the lessons of your history. Use the thought-stopping tool to interrupt worrisome loops. Affirm yourself. Investigate nutritional interventions. And let your inner wisdom be your guide moment to moment in relationships.

In the next and final chapter of this book, you'll learn to celebrate your newfound freedom, fulfillment, and fabulous good fortune. Meet me there when you're ready!

✻✻✻ ✻✻✻

Chapter 14

CELEBRATE YOUR NEWFOUND FREEDOM, FULFILLMENT, AND FABULOUS GOOD FORTUNE

*C*ongratulations! You've arrived at the final chapter of *The Gift of Betrayal.* You have, by now, begun to master or answer 13 of the 14 lessons and questions necessary to healing your life. While I hope you've learned something useful from each chapter, you've probably found that some of the lessons touched you where you most needed to be healed, while others didn't resonate for you just yet. Remember that healing is a self-paced process! And there's a personal right path for you to heal your life. As I mentioned in the Introduction, each one of us feels, sees, and grows in our own blessedly unique way. So, be gentle and patient with yourself. Revisit the lessons and work with the tools of each chapter as the fancy strikes you. Cultivate trust! You'll get just what you need, when you need it!

Now that you've arrived at the final chapter, it's time to celebrate what you've been given and what you've accomplished, because no matter where you are in life, I'm sure you neglect to do this as often as you should. I've devoted a whole chapter to celebration in order to help you remember and acknowledge its significance. So . . . what are you actually supposed to *do?* What does it mean to "celebrate your newfound freedom, fulfillment, and fabulous good fortune"?

Remember the lesson of Chapter 8: to slow down so you can examine and honor all your involvements? You worked on *being* as opposed to *doing,* on resting and relaxing, and on examining your prior balance-counterbalance structure so you could create the edifice that would best serve you *now.* You'll be drawing on some of those lessons in this chapter. In celebrating your newfound freedom, fulfillment, and fabulous good fortune, you also have to stop your running, rushing, worrying, thinking about tomorrow, and planning. But you must go *beyond* being present to the gift of the moment in another way: you're to actually *acknowledge* your accomplishments, freedom, and fortune!

Many of us repeatedly skip over this recognition-and-acknowledgment step in our lives. We push ourselves to the max in order to achieve amazing feats. Then, as soon as we master those challenges or meet our goals, we run off to tackle the next hurdles on our paths. We're constantly pushing. We're on treadmills we can't seem to get off. We neglect to pause, even for a moment, to register the magnitude of our triumphs or blessings. There's always more to do.

One of my favorite songs is "Celebration" by Kool & the Gang. It's such an uplifting reminder of the importance of partying, celebrating good times, getting our bodies moving, and having fun. We don't celebrate the good times enough. And without celebration, our lives become devoid of fulfillment and joy. Often in my workshops I have all the participants stand up, sing, and dance to the "Celebration" song. By the time it's a third of the way through, most of the people in the room are smiling and laughing. "Celebration" serves as a fabulous reminder and opening for a talk about health, fulfillment, balance, and meaning. Healing requires us to acknowledge what works!

Accomplishments Exercise

So, I suggest you pause for a while to reflect on your accomplishments. What have you struggled to achieve, surmount, or let go of? Whatever you've created until now is amazing in some way! Also, you've surely survived and thrived under extreme stress. List at least six achievements. Feel free to use the list of subjects that follows to help you. *Be sure* to write down your own triumphs in as much detail as you can!

I've Had Successes in the Following Areas:

- Self-care
- Relationships
- Parenting
- Finances
- Outlook/attitude
- Professional life
- Spiritual path
- Sports
- Recreation
- House/home
- Friendships
- Letting go
- Moving on
- Taking risks
- Banishing doubt or blame

- Cultivating acceptance
- Writing
- Building
- Singing
- Speaking
- Teaching
- Learning
- Loving
- Praying
- Dancing
- Planning
- Delivering
- Receiving
- Trusting
- Healing

I'd like to give you an example to clarify this accomplishments exercise. Patty, a 46-year-old woman who had done fabulous growth work, was sitting in my office one day feeling pretty down on herself. In the moment, she was having trouble seeing that she'd made *any* progress! So I had her do this exercise. Here are the six accomplishments she wrote down:

1.   *Four years ago I discovered that my professor husband of 19 years was having sex with the college students he was teaching. I took care of myself when my world exploded. I sought therapy, filed for divorce, and went back to school so I could change careers.*

2.   *I've gotten A's and B's in all the courses (six total) I've taken so far.*

3.   *I've become financially responsible for the first time in my life. I spend only what I earn or receive in alimony. I have no more credit-card debt.*

4.   *I've begun to explore dating.*

5.   *I've stopped blaming him for hurting me.*

6.   *I've had the courage to paint my bedroom a shocking color—and I love it!*

When Patty finished her list, I had her read it aloud. Together, we acknowledged the magnitude of her growth in four years' time. She'd initially been in a desperate state. She had survived it, learned from it, and ultimately taken charge of her life.

Looking at her list, Patty was able to see the gift of her betrayal. Doing the accomplishments exercise enabled her to reflect on her history and take stock of her growth. She recalled that she'd been a pleaser and a peacemaker in her marriage. But she hadn't been *happy!* Her newfound freedom, granted by the demise of her marriage, had enabled her to achieve a level of personal fulfillment that she'd never before experienced. She was happier than she'd ever been . . . so surely this was a cause for celebration!

Patty and I used the remainder of our time together that day to plan one. For my patient, that meant inviting three of her closest friends to join her for dinner at her favorite Mexican restaurant. She decided to share her list with them over a pitcher of margaritas. She would toast her growth and their support of her! This felt like a fitting acknowledgment for a job well done!

How can you apply the lesson of Patty's story to your own accomplishments exercise? Start to think about that. There's a personal right answer for you, too! Once you've created your accomplishment list, I suggest you share it with those who love and support you. Ask your female friends, and anyone else you think might be of help, to add their observations to your list. What have they seen you achieve? What might you be minimizing that others view as amazing feats? What else do you need to recognize? Spend as much time as you wish creating this list . . . but don't get off track. This is an exercise you're meant to do over and over and over again.

Acknowledging and celebrating your successes, small and large, in an ongoing way is the point. So how can you regularly do that? Might you benefit from creating a celebration ritual or party now? If so, create one! And have a *great time!* There are moments when a huge acknowledgment is in order, but not all accomplishments demand, or warrant, a party. So what else might you do?

Acknowledgment Journal

I personally like using gratitude journals to mark what matters. You may already be familiar with this concept. It involves keeping a daily journal and taking time each day to write down something you're grateful for. Each evening before bed, or first thing in the morning before you start your day, is often the best time. For the lesson of this chapter, I suggest you keep an "acknowledgment journal." Write something you've achieved that you're grateful to have been able to do . . . and follow it with a description of its significance. Here are some examples of *achievement/acknowledgment statements* written by others who have traveled a road similar to the one you're on now:

- *I'm grateful to have been able to drop off my son at my ex's house and avoid arguing with him. That was a lot of growth for me!*

- *I celebrate my decision to fire an attorney who demeans me. That took a lot of courage.*

- *I'm glad to have made it through today without eating tons of junk food. I've been using chocolate and cookies as self-medication for a long time!*

- *I'm grateful to have friends I can count on. I called someone for support today, and she was so helpful. I wouldn't have been able to reach out in that way before. I'm really growing!*

- *I'm so glad I avoided getting sucked in by my ex today. He tried to get me to concede on a financial matter by complimenting me and lying. I would have caved before. I've grown a lot! I no longer give away what's rightfully mine.*

- *I'm proud of myself. I signed up with an online dating service . . . and wrote my first profile today. I'm stepping into territory that used to scare me!*

- *For the first time ever, I let go of trying to fix a mess my son made. I've realized he needs to learn from his mistakes, and I need to let go of control!*

- *I asked a guy to meet me for coffee today . . . and he said yes! Yippee! I would never have done that before.*

- *I decided to stop seeing a guy after three dates. There's no chemistry with him. In the past, I would have stayed.*

- *I chose to avoid the victim role today. When I heard that my legal fees would escalate for a long time, I reminded myself that this was the price I needed to pay for freedom. I used to allow my financial worries to keep me in prison. No more!*

- *I let go of the need to be right in a disagreement with my sister. I've been unwilling to do that before.*

- *I apologized to a friend for something I did to hurt him a long time ago. He'd forgiven me, but I'd been carrying a lot of guilt. What a relief!*

- *I gave an employee positive feedback for a job well done . . . even though doing so wasn't necessary. This was growth for me.*

- *I used the constructive criticism I was given at work today to improve my performance. In the past, I would have gotten angry. Today, I was grateful for the guidance!*

- *When I heard my inner critic attack me this morning, I was able to say "Stop it" and distract myself! I'm getting better at self-care!*

- *Earlier today, I found myself comparing my progress to my friend's. I started to feel like a failure. Then I remembered to celebrate my own successes. After listing six of them, I felt a whole lot better about <u>me!</u>*

You've just read through a list of 16 *achievement/acknowledgment statements*. Each writer benefited from the exercise. You can, too! I urge you to begin the daily practice of keeping an acknowledgment journal. In doing so, you'll be forced to slow down, pay attention to both your experiences and responses, and celebrate your accomplishments—however small! In reality, there are no "small" growth steps. Even the tiniest of shifts in behavior can move mountains!

Free at Last

Yes, you're free, and you're supposed to celebrate this gift. But when you've been burned, betrayed, and consumed by fear, it can be hard to see the blessing in your newfound freedom. In fact, it can be difficult to experience your loss as liberation at all. When your dreams die, it's so easy to get stuck in hurt, anger, fear, and pain. It's common to have doubts about what your life can be. Your fears can stay alive even when the actual risk to you has gone away. It's challenging to celebrate your liberation when you don't feel free or know how your life is going to turn out.

Yet, in working through the lessons in this book, you've learned a lot about taking charge of your life. You now know what you can do to stay out of fear, doubt, the victim role, and self-sabotage. You've discovered many of the tools available to you for creating your heart's desire. You've received a lot of guidance on how to quiet your worried mind. You know what actions you need to take to heal your life!

You've discovered that you're not a victim. You're free to create the life you want. Your old beliefs have kept you in prison, but you don't need to let them be your wardens anymore. You're now free to manifest your heart's desire. And you *can* succeed! There's a universe of support available to help you if you open yourself up to its gifts!

So how are you to remember that you're fabulously free? Well, you must actively remind yourself of that fact! I suggest you thank the universe each and every day for your gift of freedom. You can make a list of all the benefits of your liberation. You might choose to recite affirmations or prayer statements, read poetry, or revisit the greatest speeches and essays of all time. Consider Martin Luther King, Jr.'s "I have a dream" speech, which ends with the words *free at last*. You can also sing songs like Sammy Davis, Jr.'s "I've Gotta Be Free" and then add *I am free . . . and I'm glad to be me* to it. In singing those words, you'll actually step into the freedom experience! You'll be reminded that you're unfettered and that it's good to be there.

I suggest you let your friends help you with this "free at last" lesson, too. They can remind you of the blessing of your current state and reassure you of your freedom and safety when your old tapes get going. Let me give you an example of what I mean.

Sandra had been married to Max, a charming yet highly dangerous sociopath, for 17 years, but she hadn't known the truth about him. For years, she'd been deceived and betrayed. Unbeknownst to her until her life exploded, he had repeatedly put her at grave risk by engaging in highly promiscuous sexual behavior. He'd also stolen money from her and many of her friends. Two years before, she'd finally gotten out. She divorced Max, gained sole custody of their children, and worked out a financial settlement that was adequate for her kids' care.

It had been over a year since she and Max had spoken to one another. She'd avoided conversing with him as much as possible. One day, she learned that he'd just stolen money from another one of her naïve friends. The next day when her ex-husband dropped their son off at home, Max waited until Sandra came to the door to tell her that he was proud of her. He'd learned that she'd been given an award in the community. He called her "honey" and said a few additional caring but clearly insincere things to Sandra. He neglected to mention the theft.

Sandra found herself really rattled for several hours. She realized how easy it had been to get sucked in by Max's attempts to be charming. She'd felt drawn to him and was later horrified. He was a dangerously attractive con man and cheat. She couldn't calm down. She called her friend Zoe for support.

"Sweetie," Zoe said, "Max can't hurt you anymore. There's nothing he can do to you. You're free!"

Upon hearing those words, Sandra began to cry with relief. She found herself saying, "I guess I needed to hear that. Even though I know what you said is true in my head, my body still responds like it used to. I feel better now. Thank you."

Sandra needed to be reminded by her friend Zoe that she was free, safe, and in charge of her own destiny. The clarifying support was liberating! It enabled her to calm down and reclaim her power. You, too, will benefit from the clarifying, loving support of friends. You're fabulously free! Claim your liberation, and let yourself celebrate it!

The Upside of Your Down

I just read an essay in the *New York Times* by a woman who found her funny, humorous side emerge after she was diagnosed with a highly aggressive form of cancer 12 years earlier. In the essay, she states that when she was threatened with losing everything that mattered, she realized that she didn't need to keep acting so grown-up! She could be silly, playful, childlike, unbridled, and free. She chose to live fully and happily in the moment and stopped worrying about what the fallout would be.

As I read her words, I found myself envisioning joyful children splashing paint all over themselves as they stood at easels for the first time. I heard the crash of falling towers of blocks built by youngsters in order to knock them down. I even saw my childhood self jumping in puddles and laughing as water splattered everywhere.

The lesson of that *New York Times* essay resonates with the lesson of this chapter. We all have so much to celebrate in *this* moment. And the more we let go of our attachment to worry, expectation, and self-doubt, the easier it becomes for us to allow our uninhibited, hopeful, joyful selves to emerge. We can all be happy right now . . . and we *need* to be!

Although the author of the essay didn't make a connection between her survival from cancer and her decision to let loose, I wonder if she helped herself heal by choosing to joke her way through the treatment and recovery. Whether she did or not, her approach surely made the chemotherapy experience more bearable. And she must have spread a little bit of joy around in the process!

No matter where you are right now in your healing journey, there's an upside to your "down." You can find something to relish in every moment. Maybe it's the kindness of friends and strangers, the fresh peach on your kitchen counter, or the rose that just opened in your garden. Maybe it's your new kitten's purr, the sun shining on your cheeks, or a beautiful song on the radio. Notice what brings you pleasure right now. What's the upside to your down?

I have found, and studies have shown it to be true over and over again, that the way we approach our lives determines our experience. If we choose to celebrate our newfound freedom, fulfillment, and fabulous good fortune, we'll experience an abundance of gratitude, joy, and grace. From our places of pleasure, we draw to ourselves and manifest all that we intend. In choosing joy, light, hope, and faith, we create and live our hearts' desires. We grasp the gift in our betrayals. We transform and heal our lives!

In Closing

As I end this final chapter, I want to remind you of its key teachings:

Slow down and acknowledge your accomplishments. Remind yourself to celebrate what works. Use tools like the accomplishments exercise, the acknowledgment journal, and the "free at last" lesson. Find the upsides to your downs. And allow yourself to grasp the gift in your betrayal. You can heal your life, and I *know* you'll do so!

Congratulations. You've just finished learning the 14 key questions and lessons necessary to healing your life after betrayal. You'll need to revisit and work with them repeatedly, but you've come a long way in healing yourself already. I'm proud of your accomplishments.

In the Afterword that follows this chapter, you'll have a chance to review the lessons in this book. After revisiting each one, you'll create your own mission statement for today. Remember, it may change as you go forward. You create your heart's desire one moment at a time. I believe in you and your fabulous future. I can't wait to hear how you're doing!

Afterword

It's time for you to review each of the 14 key lessons and questions that you've just learned. Read through each one as listed below and think about what you want to do to work with it and incorporate its message at this moment in time. You might find it helpful to revisit the appropriate chapters to refresh your memory. Record your observations and plans for implementing each *healing your life* lesson or question in the space provided or on a separate piece of paper.

1. What is betrayal, how does it feel, and where can it take you?

2. You have a choice: do you seize your power or become the victim?

3. Could you have been married to (or involved with) a sociopath?

4. How did you get here, and what are you meant to learn from this?

    _____

    _____

5. What is the role of forgiveness in healing?

    _____

    _____

6. Trust in your ability to create your heart's desire.

    _____

    _____

7. Take action to create the life you really want.

    _____

    _____

8. Slow down: examine and honor all of your involvements

    _____

    _____

9. Take risks, try new things . . . and pay attention to how you feel.

    _____

    _____

10. Let your female friends help you.

    _____

    _____

11. Learn what men have to offer and what they cannot do for you.

    _____

    _____

12. Invite joy, pleasure, and passion into your life.

    _____

    _____

13. Stay present to the gift of the moment.

    _____

    _____

14. Celebrate your newfound freedom, fulfillment, and fabulous good fortune.

    _____

    _____

Now review your reflections and write your personal "I Choose to Heal My Life" mission statement on the next page or on another a piece of paper.

I Choose to Heal My Life

In reviewing my history, I realize that I need and want to do the following:

_____

_____

_____

_____

I understand that my needs and plan will change over time. I commit to working on what I've written now, and to altering my mission statement as it makes sense to do so in the future.

I can take charge of my life. I grasp the gift of my betrayal. I heal my life. I create and live my heart's desire!

Now, make some copies of your "I Choose to Heal My Life" mission statement. Post them in a few prominent places, and carry one with you wherever you go. Read and work with the lessons daily, updating and changing them as you heal and grow. In this way you will take charge of your life and create your heart's desire. You'll grasp the gift of your betrayal, overcome your challenges, and find fulfillment. You're amazing and deserve the life you want! My hopes and prayers are with you.

Acknowledgments

$\mathcal{I}$n the past, with every manuscript I have submitted to my publisher, I've been moved to acknowledge those individuals who've played a significant role in its creation and birth. Often I couldn't wait to thank them in writing!

But in submitting *The Gift of Betrayal,* I've had a different experience. While there are many individuals to thank, I haven't wanted to create a section with a beginning, middle, and end. For the very first time, I know that the story isn't over. The real "gift" of betrayal has only just begun. And while the manuscript is finished, the journey is nowhere near its conclusion. Many more angels will enter my life to guide me, support me, and teach me what I've still got to learn. And some of my best teachers will be those who hurt me, those who lead me into the deepest pain, and those who open the doors to my own great wisdom and understanding.

Thomas Wieber, my fabulous new husband, has said, "We both needed to go through our horrible first marriages to learn to appreciate one another as we do." And I couldn't agree with him more. That begs the question: Do I thank those who have brought me pain, betrayal, hurt, fear, and ultimately wisdom? Does that even make sense? I don't really think so. But I do need to acknowledge the gift of the pain, betrayal, and transformation.

In the Dedication and throughout the text of *The Gift of Betrayal,* I've acknowledged many of those who've helped me survive, grow, and thrive through this challenging time. And there are many more unsung heroes. In fact, I'm afraid of leaving someone out if I try to list them all. So, for the first time in my writing career, I won't try to thank everyone. I'm committed to continuing to acknowledge those who help me in person whenever I can. We all need to do that more often.

However, there are a few acknowledgments I must make. First and foremost, I must thank Martha Watson. Martha was my neighbor in northern New Jersey when I was 16 years old. She was an English teacher who taught me how to write an essay! Until that point, no one had even taught me about the importance of a theme, the role of a topic sentence and supporting points in a paragraph, or the need for a conclusion. I was in high school and didn't know how to write a paper! How far I've come . . . in no small measure thanks to Ms. Martha Watson!

Second, I must thank the love of my life, Thomas Wieber, for holding me and seeing me through the most challenging chapter of my life. And I am endlessly grateful to God for bringing my intended to me when I least expected him to appear.

Third, I am overwhelmed with awe and respect for all the friends and colleagues who chose to read my manuscript and write testimonials for me. Their names follow their comments at the beginning of the book.

Fourth, I must mention a few champions of my work and teachings who remain behind the scenes. They are great gifts in my life. Thank you, Roberta Grace, Diane Ray, and Donna Abate. You rock!

And, finally, I extend my greatest gratitude to my patients and readers . . . for each of you, more than anyone else, push me to be my best self, to learn, to grow, and to give and receive. Without you, *The Gift of Betrayal* would not exist! Thank you all. And God bless you.

— **Eve A. Wood, M.D.**

About the Author

$\mathcal{E}$ve A. Wood, M.D., is Clinical Associate Professor of Medicine at the University of Arizona Program in Integrative Medicine. A practicing psychiatrist, author, speaker, and consultant, Dr. Wood is a pioneer in the field of integrative psychiatry. Having spent nearly two decades and over 30,000 hours in the care of troubled individuals from all walks of life, she has developed a treatment approach that involves traditional psychiatric medicine, psychology, and universal spiritual principles. Her method has attracted attention and acclaim from the nation's leading authorities in the fields of medicine, health, and spiritual well-being.

Dr. Wood is the award-winning author of the books *There's Always Help; There's Always Hope* and *10 Steps to Take Charge of Your Emotional Life,* as well as *The Stop Anxiety Now Kit* and the *What Am I Feeling, and What Does It Mean?* kit. She writes a column for *Massage Therapy Journal,* hosts a radio show on **HayHouseRadio.com®**, and teaches at workshops nationwide. Uniting body, mind, and spirit with a series of In One® tools, she helps individuals take charge of their emotional lives.

When Dr. Wood's life exploded in betrayal, she used the same life-affirming, integrative, and empowering tools she has learned and been teaching for years in order to heal her own life. She is now married to the man of her dreams, lives in Tucson with her husband and children, maintains a small clinical and consulting practice, and teaches at the University of Arizona Medical School.

To learn more about Dr. Wood, please visit:
www.DrEveWood.com.

For more details about this book and to share
online with your friends, please visit:
www.TheGiftofBetrayal.com.

HAY HOUSE TITLES OF RELATED INTEREST

YOU CAN HEAL YOUR LIFE, the movie,
starring Louise L. Hay & Friends
(available as a 1-DVD program and an expanded 2-DVD set)
Watch the trailer at: **www.LouiseHayMovie.com**

THE SHIFT, the movie, starring Dr. Wayne W. Dyer
(available as a 1-DVD program and an expanded 2-DVD set)
Watch the trailer at: **www.DyerMovie.com**

✻ ✻ ✻

THE AGE OF MIRACLES: Embracing the New Midlife,
by Marianne Williamson

*THE ART OF EXTREME SELF-CARE: Transform Your Life One
Month at a Time,* by Cheryl Richardson

HAPPILY EVEN AFTER: Can You Be Friends After Lovers?
by Alan Cohen

HAPPINESS NOW!: Timeless Wisdom for Feeling Good FAST, by
Robert Holden, Ph.D.

*HOW TO GET WHAT YOU REALLY, REALLY, REALLY, REALLY
WANT,* by Dr. Wayne W. Dyer and Deepak Chopra, M.D. (2-CD set)

*IF I CAN FORGIVE, SO CAN YOU: My Autobiography of How I
Overcame My Past and Healed My Life,* by Denise Linn

*INNER PEACE FOR BUSY WOMEN: Balancing Work, Family,
and Your Inner Life,* by Joan Z. Borysenko, Ph.D.

MARS/VENUS CARDS, by John Gray (50-card deck)

THE SECRET PLEASURES OF MENOPAUSE, by
Christiane Northrup, M.D.

STOP WONDERING IF YOU'LL EVER MEET HIM: A Revolu-tionary Approach for Putting the Date Back into Dating, by Ryan Browning Cassaday and Jessica Cassaday, Ph.D.

TRUST YOUR VIBES: Secret Tools for Six-Sensory Living, by Sonia Choquette

WHAT IS YOUR SELF-WORTH?: A Woman's Guide to Validation, by Cheryl Saban, Ph.D.

All of the above are available at your local bookstore, or may be ordered by contacting Hay House (see last page).

Notes

Notes

Notes

Notes

Notes

Notes

Notes

Notes

We hope you enjoyed this Hay House book. If you'd like to receive a free catalog featuring additional Hay House books and products, or if you'd like information about the Hay Foundation, please contact:

Hay House, Inc.
P.O. Box 5100
Carlsbad, CA 92018-5100

(760) 431-7695 or (800) 654-5126
(760) 431-6948 (fax) or (800) 650-5115 (fax)
www.hayhouse.com® • www.hayfoundation.org

Published and distributed in Australia by: Hay House Australia Pty. Ltd., 18/36 Ralph St., Alexandria NSW 2015 • *Phone:* 612-9669-4299 *Fax:* 612-9669-4144 • www.hayhouse.com.au

Published and distributed in the United Kingdom by: Hay House UK, Ltd., 292B Kensal Rd., London W10 5BE • *Phone:* 44-20-8962-1230 *Fax:* 44-20-8962-1239 • www.hayhouse.co.uk

Published and distributed in the Republic of South Africa by: Hay House SA (Pty), Ltd., P.O. Box 990, Witkoppen 2068 *Phone/Fax:* 27-11-467-8904 • orders@psdprom.co.za • www.hayhouse.co.za

Published in India by: Hay House Publishers India, Muskaan Complex, Plot No. 3, B-2, Vasant Kunj, New Delhi 110 070 *Phone:* 91-11-4176-1620 • *Fax:* 91-11-4176-1630 • www.hayhouse.co.in

Distributed in Canada by: Raincoast, 9050 Shaughnessy St., Vancouver, B.C. V6P 6E5 • *Phone:* (604) 323-7100 *Fax:* (604) 323-2600 • www.raincoast.com

Tune in to **HayHouseRadio.com®** for the best in inspirational talk radio featuring top Hay House authors! And, sign up via the Hay House USA Website to receive the Hay House online newsletter and stay informed about what's going on with your favorite authors. You'll receive bimonthly announcements about: Discounts and Offers, Special Events, Product Highlights, Free Excerpts, Giveaways, and more!
www.hayhouse.com®